PRAISE FOR TROUBLED

"In *Troubled*, Kenneth R. Rosen is the exact right Conrad to take us into the heart of this immense darkness. Rosen's insight, rigor, and sympathy ensure this book will stand as the definitive treatment of this troubled, troubling industry. An experience you won't forget."
—Darin Strauss, author of *Half a Life* and *The Queen of Tuesday*

"*Troubled* is a searing chronicle of the unfortunate era of 'tough love' programs for wayward American youth, told with detail and compassion, as well as an eloquent kind of well-merited rage."
—Luke Mogelson, contributing writer at the *New Yorker*

"*Troubled* by Kenneth R. Rosen is the first book written by a survivor to investigate the longer-term outcomes of adolescents who were subjected to this 'treatment' . . . If you are a parent considering seeking help for your teenager or a program survivor, I urge you to read this book and heed its lessons."
—Maia Szalavitz, author of *Help at Any Cost*

"Profoundly unsettling, *Troubled* reveals a tough-love industry in disarray. Kenneth R. Rosen combines brilliant reporting skills and brutal firsthand experience in this captivating read."
—Michael Harris, author of *Solitude* and *The End of Absence*

"Kenneth R. Rosen is a relentless reporter, and he provides a piercing view inside the disturbing, largely unregulated teen-rehabilitation industry. Rosen ensures you ask the question of what we're doing to our nation's children and who, and what, is in fact 'troubled.'"
—Sylvia A. Harvey, author of *The Shadow System*

"A vivid and eye-opening plea for reform. Rosen writes as a journalist, but also from personal experience, about getting 'kidnapped' to live in the strange world of teenage behavioral boot camps—which is an industry in America with its own unsavory logic."

—Michael Scott Moore, author of *The Desert and the Sea*

"*Troubled* investigates the unregulated Wild West of programs that claim to treat delinquent teenagers but actually further traumatize and harm them. From wilderness programs to residential treatment centers, these institutions prey on desperate parents who believe their children can be scared straight. Kenneth Rosen's heartbreaking, deeply reported book should be required reading for parents, therapists, educators, school consultants, and anyone concerned about the most vulnerable in our society: our children. *Troubled* follows four teens through four different programs, keenly documenting the resultant physical and mental abuse from those entrusted with their care. With a journalist's eye and a former troubled teen's heart, Rosen makes a powerful case for eliminating this cruel part of the school-to-prison pipeline. A powerful, revealing expose."

—Katherine Reynolds Lewis, author of
The Good News About Bad Behavior

TROUBLED

ALSO BY KENNETH R. ROSEN

Bulletproof Vest

TROUBLED

THE FAILED PROMISE
OF AMERICA'S BEHAVIORAL
TREATMENT PROGRAMS

KENNETH R. ROSEN

Published by Little A, New York

www.apub.com

Amazon, the Amazon logo, and Little A are trademarks of Amazon.com, Inc., or its
affiliates.

ISBN-13: 9781542007887 (hardcover)
ISBN-10: 1542007887 (hardcover)

ISBN-13: 9781542022118 (paperback)
ISBN-10: 1542022118 (paperback)

Cover design by Zoe Norvell

A portion of this book originally appeared, in a slightly different form, in Narratively.

Printed in the United States of America

First edition

For the troubled, in trouble, and once troubled

Life is short, though I keep this from my children.
Life is short, and I've shortened mine
in a thousand delicious, ill-advised ways,
a thousand deliciously ill-advised ways
I'll keep from my children. The world is at least
fifty percent terrible, and that's a conservative
estimate, though I keep this from my children.
For every bird there is a stone thrown at a bird.
For every loved child, a child broken, bagged,
sunk in a lake. Life is short and the world
is at least half terrible, and for every kind
stranger, there is one who would break you,
though I keep this from my children. I am trying
to sell them the world. Any decent realtor,
walking you through a real shithole, chirps on
about good bones: This place could be beautiful,
right? You could make this place beautiful.

—*Maggie Smith, "Good Bones"*

CONTENTS

A NOTE FROM THE AUTHOR

The events in this book are real. The characters who are central to this narrative—Hazel, Mark, Avery, and Mike—were chosen after interviewing more than one hundred former clients, child psychologists, counselors, and staff who spent time in "tough love" or "behavior modification" programs ranging from wilderness therapy programs to residential treatment centers and juvenile delinquent halls and beyond. These four young adults best represent a great deal of the teenagers admitted to these programs and the paths they follow into adulthood.

The reporting for this book began in 2007, when I was a teenager. Over the next year, I was admitted to three therapeutic treatment programs for adolescents in New York, Massachusetts, and Utah. In total, I was incarcerated for 288 days. These programs were known for their exploratory approach to therapy, which amounted to a brutal, forced redirection of wayward teenagers. They focused on breaking us down, but as one former client told me, "They were never as good at building us back up." For me, as for many others, the programs were the start of a life spent circulating through countless institutions and lockups.

Though the majority of programs mentioned in this book are today defunct, with the events described taking place between 2006 and 2010, similar programs still exist. In reaching out to dozens of former clients, to the educational consultants who funneled children into programs like these across the country, to parents who felt defeat in needing to resort to these programs, I found that few were willing to speak to me—even as a former client myself. Others wanted their stories told with the caveat that I not reveal their identities; thus, I have changed the names of those who were juveniles and victims. I have not altered the names of those who were charged or convicted of a crime, or anyone who has a publicly documented history of associating with the programs. I have changed the names of Hazel and Avery and composited some of the secondary and tertiary characters throughout the book to protect their privacy.

I wrote and reported for this book using all available sources: handwritten notes and letters, emails, text and encrypted messages, in-person and phone interviews, journals kept by former clients, law enforcement and autopsy reports, court records and psychological evaluations, congressional reports and state investigation materials, brochures, almanacs, private and public video recordings, literature and guides distributed to parents and clients at the programs, and testimonials given both online and off. The writing is also informed by my own experiences and life, which at times intersected—either directly or indirectly—with many of the people mentioned hereafter, most frequently with the four main characters.

—Kenneth R. Rosen
2019, Peterborough, New Hampshire

PROLOGUE

As they approach their teenage years, their lives turn. They often skip school, and when they do attend class, they find it boring and drift apart from their peers. They storm off, stiff with indignation, teachers shouting at their backs. They gravitate toward a group much older than themselves, more jaded. They meet people who see the world in the same weary way. Nothing matters. It is what it is.

As in school, they find boredom at home. Their parents are overbearing, their homes stifling. They want to live, but everything hinders their very existence. They see in their parents' lives something they can never replicate and do not want: safety, security, money, rules.

Because of these feelings, they invariably come in contact with the police—for truancy, for drug or alcohol possession, for stoking commotion at home. Or they call the police on their own because they hate their lives at home and want to be taken someplace else. Some return to those parents, to those four walls of misery. Others are charged with criminal mischief or juvenile delinquency, but it never amounts to real criminal charges. Their actions are minor hiccups, the authorities say, and they are placed in an off-the-books corrections program to get them back on track.

But the children and the authority figures in their lives have very different conceptions of where that track is leading. The parents—doctors, lawyers, accountants, plumbers—are waiting for their wayward children to wise up and follow a path of decency and responsibility into college or the workforce. They want their children to learn the importance of honesty and integrity, to grow beyond their misbehavior. But the children believe their obstinance will set them free from the constraints under which their parents live, leading them to some greater purpose, some happiness only they understand.

When their children's behavior does not change, the parents become desperate, certain their daughter or son will do something terrible, like committing an irreversible crime. Maybe they will kill themselves. Maybe someone else.

The parents then reach out to faculty at school for help. Overwhelmed and unsure of how to help, many school officials recommend third-party educational consultants who specialize in troubled youth. Often unaccredited and operating in a nebulous legal space, few of these highly paid "consultants" hold any qualifications in psychology or therapy. They routinely suggest programs and boarding schools that do not appear on academic or criminal records as treatment programs, issuing diplomas and credits under the guise of a state-accredited institution. The schools cater to these kinds of problems: depression, anxiety, low self-esteem, anger, sexual deviance, addiction, impulse control.

Very quickly, the parents make a choice that would have once been inconceivable: they have their children vanished.

Sometimes in the middle of the night, sometimes through trickery or bribes, the parents force their children into a therapeutic program far away from home, enrolling them in a short-term solution with lasting (mostly negative) effects. These programs would indeed imbue the children with something long-term, but it would not be a correction.

These teens and their problems are everywhere, in every town and every state across this country.

Many years ago, I was one of them.

They came for me one night as I slept, in March 2007. Two strange men entered my room and awakened me, asking me to get up and get dressed quickly. They were on a schedule.

This is it, I remember thinking. *Time's up.*

It was about 2:00 a.m., and the men grew agitated when I turned away. Nuzzling my pillow, I remember thinking this couldn't be happening, not to me. I fell asleep for a moment and awoke again when one of them pulled off my covers. Grabbing one of the corners, I pulled hard and tried to bring the covers over my head to keep the lights in my room, now turned on, from waking me.

A knee pressed into the small of my back and I briefly convulsed. It did not hurt, but the helplessness was suffocating. The man seemed like he was twice my height and ten times my weight. I could feel everything, all of him, as he restrained me.

"I didn't want to do this the hard way," he said.

When he let go of my arms and stood up, the meeker man stepped closer to the bed and placed next to me a pair of my oversized jeans and a tattered T-shirt. The men reminded me of George and Lennie from *Of Mice and Men*, in both appearance and demeanor. The boss and his stalwart companion.

I sat up, rubbed my eyes, and looked around to see the endless disarray in my room. My mother called it a pigsty. Computer parts, soldering irons, nuts and bolts, cardboard boxes, and loose-leaf paper were strewn about the floor. On the walls were medals, certificates, pink tardy slips, and truancy reports. The windowsills were lined with empty beer cans and bottles, filled with cigarette butts and ash. With the exception of the two men, everything seemed as it should. Until that night, I'd been comfortable in the chaos.

They would not say where we were going or why.

"How long will we be traveling?" I asked.

"Can't tell you," Lennie replied.

"How long will I be gone?"

"Let's go," George said tersely.

"Is it out of state?"

"We're on a schedule." *You said that already.*

My mother and father peeked through a crack between the two bedroom doors. I had not seen them together since the divorce.

"Go with these men, please," my mother begged.

"Don't fight this," my father warned.

George pointed toward the door, suggesting to Lennie that my parents needed to leave. And so they did.

It was a kidnapping. My parents had hired these men to strip me from my home and deliver me to what would be the first of three treatment programs. In total, these programs cost my parents tens of thousands of dollars. At the low end, a program that consisted of hiking through the Adirondack Mountains and sporadic meetings with a therapist cost my parents more than $500 a day after an initial base tuition of $20,000 for the first month. I would be in that program for more than seventy days.

Before my kidnapping, my days varied little: I woke up late, walked to a wooded area near my high school to meet some friends, swallowed a Xanax or OxyContin, and relaxed over beers or liquor with other truant friends until the final school bell rang. No one seemed to figure out why I went to class some days (for the girls) and then simply walked out other days (mere boredom), or why I was combative and argumentative (because I was high). How I met the people who gave me ketamine, who showed me what whip-its were, I cannot remember. I'd always been a quick study.

What precipitated my final weeklong suspension and eventual expulsion from high school is a blur. In no particular order, I remember being caught smoking pot on the baseball field, throwing a teacher against a locker, choking another, and having multiple run-ins with Officer Garrity. The last time I saw him was just after midnight on New Year's Day 2007, when he threw me into an ambulance and escorted me to rehab. Unlocking the handcuffs, Garrity made a point to tell me that I was bright, that I had so much potential. Much like how I viewed everyone in the town in which we lived, I took his words as insincere, fraudulent. *You say that to every kid. You don't know me.* This all made me feel more powerful, more in control, cunning and guileful—like the person I'd always wanted to be.

As I was dragged away from my bed and shoved into a van, I felt my future vanish.

———

Though I have written briefly about my childhood troubles in the past, I have never cared to talk in depth or openly about my time in these treatment programs—a lockdown residential treatment center in Utah, a therapeutic boarding school in Massachusetts, an outdoor therapy program in New York State—because I felt ashamed. I felt ashamed that those programs, despite fair warnings against what would become of me if I did not resolve to be a better young man, did not change me. Eventually my actions, unchanged into young adulthood, led me to juvenile detention and jail sentences.

For many of those turbulent years I felt that I was strong enough to leave my experiences from those programs in my past. I believed others should be similarly strong. Those who were not strong, who let their memories of that time bring them down and out, were weaker than me and thus were broken. It took me more than a decade to learn that my initial feelings about these programs were incorrect, that they did lasting damage to me and others like me. This book aims to correct the record.

The programs—which seem on paper like any camp or preparatory school and feature dorms, a headmaster, intramural sports—include the added "benefit" of group therapy and corporal punishment. Often staffed by uncaring, overworked, and underqualified counselors, these programs are entirely unregulated by the federal government, or by the governments of the states in which they operate. Though young boys and girls remain outside the criminal justice system, they instead enter a shadowy network of institutions designed to prevent teenagers from being arrested.

Adolescence has always been turbulent, but the technological changes of the past few decades have complicated a child's most formative years in ways previous generations could never have imagined. Worldwide, between 10 and 20 percent of children in 2013 experienced a mental disorder, with an increase of over 50 percent expected by the end of 2020. Today's parents agonize about disorders and issues they never faced when they were young, and many are uncertain of how to deal with those problems in their own children. Into this void, a cottage industry has sprung up.

Those worried about drug use and dropout rates can connect with like-minded parents via internet forums, Facebook groups, and Twitter chats. They can read books such as *Far from the Tree: Parents, Children, and the Search for Identity* or *The Good News About Bad Behavior: Why Kids Are Less Disciplined Than Ever—And What to Do About It.* They can find advice and information on sites such as HelpYourTeenNow.com, teenbootcamps.org, BestTherapeuticBoardingSchools.com, TroubledTeenHelp.com, AllKindsofTherapy.com, and AnswersForParents.com. One of the most popular, according to David L. Marcus, who wrote a book about the residential treatment program Hazel would attend, is StrugglingTeens.com, which has attracted hundreds of thousands of page views from across the country. As Marcus describes, some of the posts he found on the site "hinted at heartbreaking stories"; online forums twenty years ago had subject lines that read "Help needed for 12-year-old," "16-year-old son needs rehab," "13-year-old with anorexia," "What's next for my 14-year-old truant?" "Out of control 15-year-old daughter," "'Ripping my hair out," "Teen giving up on school—help!" "How can I help this child? How can I help me?" and "What do I do?" Today, StrugglingTeens.com, which bills itself as "the original website of information on schools and programs for teens and young adults," has a much more direct tone. It endeavors to place children in programs, while providing press releases that suggest "Emotional Growth (Character) schools and programs . . . work."

In response to the clear market demand (thanks to the decline of boarding and military schools and to more-nuanced and complex cultural, political, and socioeconomic shifts), for-profit companies began opening these programs across the country. The programs are, at their core, your typical residential drug and alcohol treatment centers, but they also are unique in their charge: rather than treating or rehabilitating a child to restore them to a former self, the programs aim to forever alter the *behavior* of teenagers. Run variously by entrepreneurs and private health providers, the programs offer as an argument for existence the growing need for children to be treated for their mental illnesses before their struggles land them in prison or, worse, in the morgue. Schools in a similar vein once operated in Jamaica and the Czech Republic, though their student bodies were composed mostly of American children. Tough muscular men and women, called "escorts" or "transporters," were hired to bring struggling kids to these programs from around the globe. Their parents felt, much as my parents felt, that they had no other choice.

One such desperate parent, a woman named Jackie, recently wrote to me. She had read my past writing in the *New York Times* about the ranch I was sent to in Utah, and she wanted my advice about her sixteen-year-old daughter, whom I'll call "Mary." Mary had stolen her mother's car and driven it while under the influence. She had lived with strangers with whom she traded sex for drugs, her mother believed. Mary spoke to her mother as if she were an ATM—only when she needed cash.

Like my mother and father, Jackie had decided to send Mary away to a treatment program that promised to rid her teenager of bad habits and poor academics. "I just didn't know how to keep her safe at home. She had no brake pedal," Jackie wrote. "She wasn't scared of anything."

What she sought from me, though, was not insight into my familiarity with these institutions. She instead wanted to share how tough the last few years had been for her and wanted to clarify for me that she loved her daughter and only wished to save her. These programs were full of children like Jackie's: seemingly ungrateful and undisciplined children in need of a strong corrective institution. Knowing that I was once one of them, Jackie wanted my absolution for her choice. After a childhood characterized by self-harm and antisocial behavior, I now had a prestigious job and had found solace in sobriety. Something from those programs must have helped me. Right?

Any year before this conversation, I would have told Jackie that the programs were fine, despite the constant news about mistreatment and mismanagement and, sometimes, death. I would have told her stories about the many people I knew from the programs who benefited from their time away from conventional schooling, from bad influences back home, from drugs and alcohol, and who needed the therapy and resilience training and a tough hand every now and again. I would have told her that she had made the right decision and should not lose any more sleep. I would have told her that, rest assured, her child would—like myself—end up fine.

Around this time, though, I learned about the deaths of many who had attended those programs with me. Every so often, I would log onto Facebook and voyage through the comments and posts in one of the "survivor" groups I had joined, like a distant land unrecognizable to me ten years since my last program. There were different groups for different programs, all recalling the time members spent in tough-love treatment. Then obituaries began to appear almost weekly across these groups. Each new, premature death took me back to a time when we were all filled with worry and helplessness. I began to rethink everything I had told myself and others about the effects the programs had had on me. More important, I had a chance to revisit how those programs had affected others.

Before Jackie, when I was confronted by a parent's pleas, desperate for insulation from their decision rather than comfort for their children, I responded with aplomb and refrain. I bit back the anger that had never slowed since—or, perhaps, in spite of—those programs, and I offered them solace. Not again.

"I believe I would have grown out of it," I wrote back to Jackie. "Things only became much worse once I came home after a year away." I recounted to her what happened after: how I was sober for six months before joining friends in an attempt to rob a gas station with an imitation gun. I finally got it together and went on to college, but years later I almost killed myself.

"I think people who write about the industry also believe that it has always been more for the parents than for the children," I ended my note.

Jackie thanked me for my insight, but clearly my words had not changed her conviction. She was, after all, speaking to someone who could have been her son. She said she was looking into other programs for her daughter anyway. She was sure that there was still hope in the system of programs into which, to use her own words, she had "sold" her daughter.

While the first few attempts weren't helpful, she seemed to breathe easy believing another program, perhaps more secluded and farther away, might make a difference.

———

All the lives chronicled in the following pages, though different in their capacities for compassion and honesty and fortune, are intertwined. Each presents a looking glass into what may have been for children admitted to these programs and, in some cases, what may still come.

At the same time there are increasing calls to regulate what teenagers can access online, these programs continue to lack regulatory oversight. This book hopes to show that in many, if not all, cases these programs do more harm than good. The programs oftentimes encourage a self-fulfilling prophecy. The stories included in this book—Hazel, Avery, Mark, and Mike—are representative of a massive industry that continues operating despite unethical and illegal practices that have gone largely ignored for years. There is no indication that these practices will change or that parents will consider state-run or evidence-based therapies that are championed as better, safer alternatives to these programs.

It is therefore my earnest hope that this book will educate and make itself useful to those in trouble, those who have been in trouble, and those seeking to pull themselves through.

BOOK I

WILDERNESS

HAZEL

1

Dear Hazel,

You have behaved in a totally unacceptable manner and have hurt and disappointed a lot of people close to you. A little lie here and another one there, dabbling in drugs and alcohol all add up to a very nasty situation . . . Much more of your life is ahead of you than behind. You have had a bumpy road through the early part of your life. Unpleasant stuff happened to take away some of the fun of growing up. Throughout all this you remained loyal to your Mom when some of us did not and you should feel good about that.

—Grandpa, excerpt from letter to Hazel

Against the bright sky, the mountain was dark and alone, and the world in its shadow appeared unlighted. Within that shadow, a group of teenage girls sat around a campfire eating bowls of bland rice and lentils. When they finished their dinner, the girls began to lick the inside of their tin cups. Everyone licked and spat, freeing the bits of rice and twig stuck to the inside of the cups. They called this "sumping." It was how they cleaned their dishes after each meal: with bodily liquids.

Hazel found the act heinous and hideous, but she was compelled to follow the rules. Hazel was a newcomer to this abstract stretch of wilderness, the site of Adirondack Leadership Expeditions (ALE), a program for troubled youth in upstate New York. So alien was this new life and crowd that Hazel almost forgot it was only a few days ago when she thought of herself as normal.

She was normal like her classmates in high school, normal like the girls on television. She dressed the way they did and talked the way they did. Sure, she partied, but the same way her classmates partied. She felt like there were a few things wrong, minor problems she had to overcome in her family or personal life, but nothing that was so extraordinary that she would not one day turn out okay. Her grandmother disagreed—which is how she wound up here, watching all these strange girls licking their tin cups.

———

From birth, Hazel had bounced from one caregiver to another. She never had a proper home, a place where she could find calm and comfort, a respite across the uneasy years of youth.

In the 1980s, her mother, Paula, gave birth to her first child, a boy, in West Orange, New Jersey, a rough stretch not far from New York City in an area that accounted for more than 60 percent of violent crimes throughout New Jersey. Paula's adopted mother hated the men her daughter dated, especially the black men. To spite her adopted mother, Paula began a relationship with a drug dealer named John. He was promptly incarcerated right before the birth of their son.

When John was finally released from prison, he moved in with Paula, who began using and dealing meth and heroin out of their house, to make rent.

"My grandma looked into the window and saw that, with my brother there, and called the cops right away," Hazel said years later. "He was a year old when she got [custody] of him."

Paula's mother took her grandson into her care and fought to keep him. She would not let him get swept up into the dealings of Paula and John, who now faced years in prison. When John was sentenced to three years in the state penitentiary, Paula returned home on a program aimed at rehabilitation. The only lesson she would take away was geographic: if you leave behind what is most troublesome, it can never follow you, a fallacy she packed into a four-door beige sedan before sinking into the realization that she had nowhere to go. So she stayed and waited, subsisting on dread and constant worry.

John would reconnect with Paula after making parole a few years later. When she learned she was pregnant with a second child, she celebrated with a six-pack of beer in her and John's small one-bedroom apartment. Rather than keep the child, it seemed more prudent to give the baby up for adoption, which is what brought Paula to the borough of Queens, New York, in February 1991, where Hazel would be born. But when she looked into her daughter's light-brown eyes, touched her dark-olive skin and even darker hair, Paula decided to abandon the adoption idea and settled down in New York City. She would keep Hazel for herself. John shortly returned to prison, after violating the conditions of his parole, so she was left to raise the little girl alone, her mind somewhat distantly occupied with thoughts of her son and the life she had but did not want.

Paula first tried to end her life a month before Hazel turned thirteen. The two of them had moved from Queens to Great Gorge, a condominium complex in Vernon, New Jersey. It was New Year's Eve 2003, and Paula was depressed and drinking heavily. Hazel was at a friend's house filming their own version of a Shakira music video: "Objection (Tango)." They dressed like Shakira, in tank tops and short skirts that unfurled as they spun. By 6:00 p.m., Paula had still not arrived to pick up her daughter, and the family hosting Hazel grew worried. They tried to call Paula several times but could not get through. Meanwhile, Paula was in their Great Gorge apartment calling her own mother in Montclair, New Jersey, to tell her that she had ingested fifty sleeping pills. She would soon be dead, she told her adopted mother, but more important, someone would need to go get Hazel.

"Happy New Year. Thankfully it will be my last," Paula said.

Paula's suicide attempt did not succeed, but a few hours later, around midnight, Hazel's grandmother and grandfather arrived at Hazel's friend's complex with Hazel's older brother, several years her senior, in the back seat. They pulled up to the house and, when invited in, found Hazel, still playing.

"I had gotten my period for the first time that day," Hazel explained to me, "and that night I moved into my grandma's house."

Hazel was forced to move in with her brother and grandparents. She transferred to Montclair to finish middle school. Though she was just a few towns away, Hazel became obsessed with making sure her mother was alive and well. If Paula did not answer the phone in the morning, Hazel would set off with her guidance counselor to go check that her mother was still alive. Hazel and the counselor would arrive outside the home, climb the stairs outside the Great Gorge apartment, and peer through the window to see inside, a musty room usually filled with ash and debris from a lonesome bacchanalia the night before.

Hazel received her first psychological evaluation that year at the behest of her grandmother. She was diagnosed with attention deficit hyperactivity disorder (ADHD) and prescribed Concerta, used to treat ADHD and narcolepsy. Her grandmother assured her that this was the best way forward. Rather than sitting down with an irrepressible teen, her grandma wanted a diagnosis to be the answer, but Hazel never felt mentally ill.

"They put me on everything and assumed a lot of things because of my mom, which was kind of fucked up," Hazel would say, "like I was a young sad kid because of what she did. There was a lot of misdiagnosis."

Hazel was often scolded for her absenteeism and continued contact with her mom, and as she entered high school, the truancy became worse. Hazel began to skip school to smoke weed with her brother, with whom she had reconnected and who acted as a local dealer. As a teen, Hazel went through phases, at one time wearing dark eyeliner and heavy jackets that obscured her petite figure, making her look more menacing. Later it would be large puffy coats made by FUBU or A Bathing Ape and baggy clothes with muted colors. Plugged into her CD Walkman and listening to hip-hop artists like Shakira, Daddy Yankee, or Pitbull, she wore earbuds constantly, even though her grandmother would nag about them blowing out her eardrums.

The pills that Hazel continued to take never worked because she would hide them beneath her tongue or between her gums and cheek, a subversion tactic known as "cheeking," showing her grandmother her mouth and pretending to have swallowed the medication. When she did take them, the schedule was erratic, never leaving enough room for the prescription to take hold and make a difference. The list of medications grew—to include Risperdal, for schizophrenia, and Trileptal, for bipolar disorder—as Hazel's grandmother went hunting for psychiatrists who could diagnose her granddaughter's defiance. "There was always a new drug that they wanted to try," Hazel said. "If someone didn't like the prescriptions, or the idea of me being on prescriptions, my grandma would fire them. She would find somebody else who would give me something."

During Hazel's freshman year in high school, her mother had moved into an apartment in Montclair, to be closer to Hazel and her brother, an apartment to which Hazel would return with friends. Paula gave them cigarettes and smoked weed with them.

"She was my friend the whole time," Hazel told me. "She kept me around to have a friend."

On the days when Hazel skipped school to hang out with her brother at their mother's, the world seemed less chaotic and unmanageable.

Everyone and everything she needed was right there in the room where they smoked and talked and played music. Hazel was fifteen when she saw her father again, in that same apartment. John emptied a Black & Mild cigarillo and packed it with marijuana. The blunt went around, from father to son to mother to daughter.

Around this age, Hazel started dating an eighteen-year-old named Simon who had graduated from their high school and was living in his car, a place of his own and something Hazel wished she had and found in him. Simon and Hazel both worked at an Italian restaurant owned by one of Paula's boyfriends. They liked the same music. They hated their guardians and wanted independence. They were in love. Youth could still be simple.

Simon and Hazel would often go to Paula's apartment, where the three now shared lines of cocaine, heads of hallucinogenic mushrooms. On October 31, 2006, Hazel left her grandmother's house to spend the day with Simon. She lied to her grandmother about where she was going, whom she was seeing, and where she was staying that night. When she returned home, her grandmother had Hazel admitted to a short-term local inpatient treatment program, reserved for substance abusers of all ages and drug preferences. "She wanted to get into everyone's life, like my mom's—very nosy, controlling, and this was just something else she could control," Hazel remembered. "She just sees my mom as a failure and sees a lot of her in me."

None of the counseling or rehabilitation programs or stints in hospital beds were new to Hazel. She had seen the inside of residential treatment facilities all her young life, once attending the outpatient program at High Focus in nearby Parsippany. "The emergency psychiatrist and therapist said in front of me, 'You should consider boarding school.'" Her grandparents did. They followed the advice of others, desperate for someone to make a decision where they could not. If the adage of parenting is that a child comes with no handbook, then it should follow that a parent writes their own.

As Hazel was getting ready to leave for another night out with Simon and friends, she noticed all her AOL Instant Messenger messages displayed on her grandmother's computer screen. Her grandmother had installed a Snoop Stick on her computer, a monitoring device that logged everything Hazel typed into her keyboard: every chat, message, note, and private journal entry came also to her grandmother.

"What do you think you're doing?" Hazel said. "Are you spying on me?"

"It's not spying," her grandmother said. "It's making sure you're making healthy decisions and spending time with the right influences."

Their wall of trust had crumbled, and a barrier of fortified secrecy rose in its place. She felt she could tell her grandmother nothing, and the consequences were severe. As she walked to school later that week, a car pulled up beside Hazel. A bunch of teenage boys rolled down the windows and got out. They surrounded her and taunted her, the details of which are hazy now for Hazel, who was outnumbered. They touched her between her legs and ran their hands across her chest. They nearly forced her into the car, but she struggled and fought back. They left in the car and she stumbled to school, looking ever more forward to the weed she would smoke, the solace she might find in the company of Simon and Paula.

When she went to report the incident to the police, they told her there was nothing they could do. They cautioned her that if she tried to name the boys, it would only make things worse for her. "Then I ended up saying I lied, which was even worse," Hazel said years later. "And to this day, yeah, my grandma, she thinks I lied." And this gave her grandmother all the ammunition she needed for the drastic changes she had in store.

———

Hazel knew her relationship with her grandmother, and by extension her grandfather, was rapidly deteriorating, but she figured they would muddle through until she turned eighteen. Then she would be on her own, unrestricted by the adults plaguing her life. But on November 6, 2006, just days after her enrollment in the short-term inpatient treatment, everything changed.

"We're going to drive you to school today," her grandmother told her.

Hazel closed the front door behind her and looked out at the driveway and the idling vehicle. Her grandpa sat behind the wheel of a gray Acura SUV. In the back seat, Paula was avoiding eye contact with her only daughter, her face a blur of tears. "I remember my mom was basically telling me with her eyes, 'Don't get in the car.'"

Hazel climbed into the back seat and leaned toward her grandmother in the front passenger seat.

"What the fuck is going on?" Hazel demanded. It was seven in the morning and the birds outside clamored. The door locks engaged, and instead of taking the usual right toward her high school, her grandpa signaled and went left.

"We're taking you to a wilderness therapy program in the Adirondacks," her grandmother said coldly, staring ahead.

Hazel lunged for the door handle, but it was too late. Her screams seemed to shake the birds off their trees as the vehicle gained speed. Hazel spat at her grandmother, tore at the seat cushions, kicked and punched the headrest where her grandpa sat pleading and pleading—his attention half on her, half on the road—to please calm down, to please know that everything will be okay and that, no, they could not let her out.

"Papa, please, please," Hazel yelled and kicked at the headrest.

"We're turning around," Grandpa said, almost relieved.

"No," Grandma said. "Drive."

Her grandpa jammed the accelerator after a slight hesitation.

Four hours later, Grandpa pulled the Acura off Route 86 in New York at a set of golden arches. Hazel had been dejected after tuning into her iPod, which Paula had slipped her along with an Ambien. "I remember singing Kelly Clarkson's 'Low.' I was just screaming, all the saddest shit," Hazel said later. "I was really dramatic. I was just really scared." At the McDonald's, she ate chicken tenders and stared out the window of the motionless car.

She was too far from home to know where she was. She could not run away. She wanted to run, back to Simon, back to her life, but at least she was with her mother, who sat beside her. They ate McDonald's together and cried, and her mother shook not from the sobbing but from her own alcohol withdrawal. Years later Hazel would say, "I had no idea what was about to happen."

Deep in Adirondack Park, at the farthest reaches of northern New York State, not far from the McDonald's, was the village of Saranac Lake, a picturesque hamlet dappled with two hundred historic low-slung timber-framed houses. After their lunch, and with little fare-well or forewarning, Grandpa, Grandma, and Paula left Hazel on the doorstep of one of those low-slung houses on Church Street. The door opened and two strangers took her by the arms and escorted her inside.

For the next few hours Hazel was shuttled between doctors—falling asleep in the waiting room because of the sleeping pill her mother had given her. She was given preventative shots, and a woman named Deborah stripped Hazel of everything she had: her clothes, her iPod, her rings and friendship bracelets, her makeup and nail polish, her identity. They swapped out her underwear for white cotton panties and made her trade the elastic hair tie she wore with one that they provided. "I couldn't have anything that was mine, and that was really sad for me," Hazel said.

They handed her a teal booklet and said she should read it once she had settled for the night, which would be in a few hours, when she reached camp. *Camp,* she thought, *what camp?* Deborah told Hazel to thumb through the booklet and to ask the instructors if she had any questions about what she read. Across the cover, framed by hand-drawn silhouettes of ridged, jagged mountains, the title read "Adirondack

Leadership Expeditions." Hazel became resigned to the reality that she had been sent to some type of boot camp for teens who did bad things. She did not know exactly what they did at these camps or schools, but she had seen them on popular television shows like A&E's *Beyond Scared Straight!* or ABC's *Brat Camp* and heard rumors of other kids who went missing and had, years later, returned with stories about strange cult-like programs in the middle of nowhere aimed at "rehabilitation." "I don't think it was for a certain type of kid, but a certain type of parent that would send their kid there. It was more like a bratty parent camp for the worried helicopter parent."

After Hazel's doctor appointments on Church Street, Deborah and a driver took Hazel out of town in a black Chevy Suburban with the door and window locks secured. The scenery blurred through the tinted windows. The white caps adorning a winter in the mountains appeared foreboding and alien. Soon the village of Saranac Lake slipped away and the trees grew higher. Hazel's breath was a rebellious cloud of steam against the tired early evening mist as the Ambien, anxiety, and fear took a stronger hold.

The roads narrowed. Suburbia ebbed into wilderness with spruce and pine and hemlock everywhere, dusted with snow. The snow rose higher against the bark the farther into the woods they traveled. Real country, deep country. They navigated a final gravel road and crossed a squat single-lane timber trestle footbridge over troubled water. But for some ice floes knocking against the shore, the creek was frozen. Hazel was tired but overcome by adrenaline and sobriety when they stopped at the center of a great big field and a different pair of strangers took her by the arms. The new duo handed her a hiking pack that she lunged onto her back and which slanted her forward. She started walking but stumbled and fell under its weight.

After hiking through thick brush and deep snow, she arrived with the new set of adults at a primitive campsite. A group of smelly girls sat around a fire, twitching in the wind, eating what appeared to be scraps of food for dinner. The girls introduced themselves one by one in their formal circle. Hazel watched the strange group of girls eat and then perform the sumping ritual, spitting into their bowls then licking them clean. Each girl wore dark rain pants and a bright-orange hooded sweatshirt under a black rain jacket. Each wore a bright-orange beanie cap, beneath which their eyes were ringed with dirt. "The orange is to make sure we aren't shot by hunters," a girl in the group whispered.

Rain fell softly, first as a mist then as a patter against the carpet of rotted leaves. After dinner, Hazel sat by the fire and fumed. It was as if the adults in her life had sent her to prison. She wondered whether she was responsible, if she was a lost cause like her mother. But Hazel was different. She was not like her mother. Or was she?

On that first night, the instructors shrugged off Hazel's many questions—"But Deborah said to ask!"—and put the children to sleep in whimsical sleeping bags under makeshift tents. An instructor demonstrated for Hazel the proper way to string taut the blue tarp that formed her shelter, though it offered little protection from the elements. A hole poked somewhere in the middle caused a trickle of rain to seep onto the sleeping bag that lay below, an indignity that further broke Hazel.

She felt an all-consuming sadness, an impenetrable darkness that loomed over her with the distant knowledge that people were out there beneath the rain and darkness, sitting by the fire, but far from her nevertheless. They weren't there for her; they were against her. These strangers were part of some distant, growing body of people who conspired to lock her up and change everything about her. Hazel admitted she needed changing. She admitted that not everything in her life up until then had been commendable or something toward which she had always wished to aspire. But it was a life, and there was time.

Now, she found she had nothing, that her life had vanished.

2

With all this baggage and, yes, the abuse that you had to take, it was only to be expected that you should stumble. Oh my!—All these metaphors for growing up . . . You may think when I talk with you that I am making light of this, Hazel . . . Your problem is you. You work on yourself . . . Get that pretty smile back on your face. Your Grandma is a fine person cast in the role of enforcer and that's not fair . . . If this is going to work out right, the self that you are has to be something worth being.

—*Grandpa, excerpt from letter to Hazel*

Although she was not taken from her home in the middle of the night as other students had been, Hazel shouldered a similar fear of abandonment. She internalized the notion that she was without support. She was without a family. Worst of all, she came to believe herself to be abnormal, a cyst on society. In this, Hazel was not unlike many of the sumping girls she held in such contempt that first night. They were all deemed to be "troubled" by their caregivers, and the program was meant to scare them straight.

Most of them were there because of issues with substance abuse. Hazel's mother and father had introduced her to drugs far earlier than most children; typically the decision to use a substance for the first time is voluntary. The rationale that drives this decision is often at the crosshairs of nature and nurture, and at the crux of this is stress. Stress is the natural response to physical, mental, or emotional challenges.

The use of substances like tobacco and nicotine, alcohol, and marijuana is often attributed to socialization. The Partnership for Drug-Free Kids has said for decades that when teens see how these products are readily available and widely enjoyed, they are normalized as a part of the teenage experience. For recreational substance use, two factors are often at play: passive peer pressure and instant gratification. Passive peer pressure is shown to be more influential than active peer pressure when it comes to getting a teen to smoke. The understated stress of imitating those around an individual often leads to mimicked behaviors, both good and bad.

What many programs for teenager therapy seem to elide and what they fail to acknowledge is the way a teen's brain is still developing. The prefrontal cortex of the human brain is not fully developed until roughly the age of twenty-five. This part of the brain is known for controlling "complex cognitive behavior, personality expression, decision making, and moderating social behavior." Because of this, teens rely on the amygdala during the decision-making process, which is a much more emotionally driven center of the brain. The inability to resist risky behaviors, coupled with the heightened sensitivity to stress, results in impulsive actions with immediate reward—an inherent teenage pathology.

In this way, the girls who surrounded Hazel were not that different from their peers, despite their particular brand of risky and impulsive behavior leading them to ALE. They had all entered a world separate from reality, in which an estimated ten to twenty thousand kids experience a furloughed youth each year, a world hidden inside privately funded, privately operated redirection treatment centers that cater to children like Hazel. Though none of the programs had been proved to work, the prospect of a simple cure for a problem child was hardly something a caregiver could ignore.

———

When I was admitted to ALE in March 2007, though in a different, all-male group apart from Hazel's group, I experienced similar feelings of social divorcement and abandonment. As I started reporting on this subject, I decided to reexamine and reevaluate my own experience. Through speaking with more than one hundred former clients like Hazel, what emerged was a portrait of an industry with humble roots, which soon became entangled in the messy world of for-profit health care. The treatment plans, honed over years of psychoanalysis of adults, became an extended laboratory for youth psychology, with many of the treatment methods going untested until actual patient therapy sessions. Those same methods were chosen not because they had proved to be effective but because they had potential.

ALE's setting is based on a romantic American idea: vast stretches of wilderness with curative powers. Wilderness therapy takes its cues from manifest destiny, adding a modicum of adventure therapy and a scantling of experiential education. The basis is simple: as in Boy Scouts or Girl Scouts, teaching children to care for themselves boosts self-esteem and confidence, allowing for the learned individualized freedom that promotes growth. It also hopes to promote the shedding of a child's antisocial and destructive singularity and any burdens of internal (mental or physical) combustion in the wilderness. Being part of a team helps a child see their own value to others and, most important, to themselves.

The psychiatric roots for the programs date to the early 1900s, when tent therapy—during which patients were isolated in nature from other patients—was often prescribed for clients suffering from psychological issues. Despite promising initial research, a substantive correlation between being outside and psychological healing was never proved, and soon all studies were dropped. A similar therapeutic approach reemerged in the 1930s, this time aimed at rowdy and inconsolable youth. Observe the youth, use experiential and adventure education to foster growth both mentally and physically, diagnose the young patient, and issue a psychotherapy treatment plan. It was an extended use of the "go play outside" refrain, with the addition of incarceration.

Adventure education is the crux of these wilderness programs, and many parents and teachers have mistaken these programs for a National Outdoor Leadership School (NOLS), a "leading source and teacher of wilderness skills and leadership that serve people and the environment," or an Outward Bound program, with its mission "to change lives through challenge and discovery." Both programs differ vastly from their therapeutic counterparts. Founded in Wales during World War II, Outward Bound transported its methods of wilderness leadership learning to the United States in the early 1960s as a cultural rise in alternative learning was being welcomed. The standard course was roughly four weeks long and included rock climbing, hiking, and time alone in the wilderness, called "solos." Where Outward Bound and NOLS are like summer camps and leadership training, the others are more like nomadic rehabilitation and detox centers.

Soon this model of self-improvement wilderness programs branched out across the country, influencing more than two hundred programs, many of which called Brigham Young University (BYU)—a Church of Jesus Christ of Latter-day Saints college—their home. A survivalist and graduate of BYU who began teaching the nuances of hunting and survival to local hunters and fishermen, Larry Dean Olsen, was tapped by the university to teach an expedition course based on Outward Bound philosophies, to embolden failing clients. Its affiliation with the Latter-day Saints meant that the program's core values were not secular, though the many Outward Bound equivalents did not adhere to Mormon ideals. The similarities between ALE's marketing and these programs may or may not have been intentional.

The psychiatric approach fell away with the rise of the more spiritual Outward Bound and BYU programs, but the emphasis on mental health made a return in the 1980s and '90s. Steve Cartisano, a chiseled, rough-hewn former military infantryman with a square jaw and stubble for a beard, took the Olsen philosophy, which he, too, had learned while attending BYU, and applied a sheen of psychological research to it. The commercial success of his institutions—privately funded wilderness excursions for "troubled teens"—would make him millions in 1988, bringing to a head an industry that otherwise remained, as one journalist wrote, "marginally solvent." The industry for sending your children away in hopes of renewal or revision had become a "cash cow."

The name "Adirondack Leadership Expeditions" was a misnomer, like much of the treatment designed to redirect "loafing" teenagers. Within a year of its founding in 1997, Aspen Education Group, which operated ALE and many similar programs, reported revenues of $28 million. A decade later, Bain Capital acquired Aspen and its subsidiaries for a reported $300 million. The company's impressive profits (estimated at 10 to 20 percent of its revenue) came from private families who turned their pockets out while under duress. Integral to this booming multibillion-dollar industry were the educational consultants, the gatekeepers whom Hazel's grandparents found through the school's guidance counselors.

Most programs today incorporate an intensive hiking regimen, corporal punishments, strict dietary restrictions, and frequent therapy sessions not only with trained therapists but also with the young, untrained adults who are recruited to lead the groups into stretches of vast wilderness alone. Many other wilderness programs encourage their clients to follow a prescribed program and use a level system to evaluate a client's progress.

At ALE, the core program was split into four phases. Hazel, like most newcomers, started at the first phase, called Turtle Phase. The shortest of the four phases, it lasted three to four days, during which Hazel had to accept her placement and focus on learning and improving communication skills. She was required to write a letter of accountability to her grandparents, noting everything she had done wrong, owning up to her mistakes. Those were known as the "soft skills." The "hard skills" would come later, during the Bear, Wolf, and Hawk Phases, and included making a digging stick, for latrines, and fashioning a walking stick, a medicine bag, deadfall critter traps, and other tools. The girls could only move to the next skill and phase when the instructors (clients were not to call them counselors, because they were instructors, they said, and were there to do that, not counsel) had signed off, an arbitrary advancement that many clients felt, in hindsight, stagnated any real chance for growth.

The length of the phases varied depending on each girl's motivation, her determination, and the belief that toeing the line would send her home. Though most girls wended through Turtle Phase in four days, Hazel took only a day to complete the first set of tasks. Once the instructor signed off and Hazel received her Impact Letter—a letter from her grandparents that outlined why she was sent away and what they expected from her next—she could graduate from Turtle 'Phase and continue through the series of phases she would need to complete before going home. Following Turtle Phase, Bear Phase—which included another set of hard and soft skills—focused on discovering strengths, habits, and patterns and becoming responsible for personal choices, trap and cordage making, fire starting. Wolf Phase focused on relationship building and advanced communication skills. Hawk Phase taught the teens to internalize healthy coping skills to reinforce positive thinking and success through group leadership, a phase rarely reached.

Much of the symbolism behind the phases—Turtle, Bear, Wolf, Hawk—was influenced by the Oneida people, a founding tribe of the

Iroquois, whose name translated into the People of the Upright Stone and who were part of a short history outlined in the teal book, the Growth Book, carried everywhere by Hazel and the other girls. If a girl lost her Growth Book, it meant she was negligent and irresponsible and in need of correction. What she could eat might be restricted, or she would be ordered to dig the group latrine (two feet wide, four feet deep, using her hands and her digging stick) or to present a lecture to the group on the dangers of being unorganized.

The Growth Book explained meaning behind the phases. The turtle symbolized the earth and a wholesome treatment of, or respect for, the land and its use. The shell of a turtle represented the founding principle behind living things: life grew from within a shell. Turtles carry their homes on their backs, are reserved and shy, and are very cautious when confronted. They do not like surprises. As a matrilineal tribe, the Oneida people further believed that the turtle carried the weight of the world on its shell, much like Atlas carried our planet, a sort of examiner at a distance from the whole. In this way, they interacted with the Bear and Wolf clans to analyze problems within a group. Turtles are learned at patience and perseverance. Bears show restraint over impulse. Wolves use their senses and pragmatism as they approach problems and hurdles, learning to be more watchful and in some cases more silent—the quieter they become, the more they hear. Hawks rise and overcome.

The Growth Book also contained smaller instructional guides on the tasks that were needed to complete each phase: how to make knots and distinguish meadow-mouse tracks from gray-squirrel tracks, bear paws from marten paws. It explained at length the Leave No Trace wilderness policy, which outlined ways to preserve the wilderness as it is, and general program rules such as no cursing or fighting. The Serenity Prayer and poems like Robert Frost's "The Road Not Taken" were scattered throughout its pages.

Most other wilderness programs are similarly therapeutic and self-help in nature, providing an overwhelming litany of therapeutic sayings and mnemonic devices (KISS for Keep It Simple, Stupid and SMART goals for Specific, Measurable, Achievable, Realistic, and Timely). ALE approached therapy like any contemporary wilderness program: a mix of therapies went into daily activities, subtly and many without the direct knowledge of the clients, because change takes attrition.

But what the psychiatric, self-help approach overlooks is the potential for physical harm that cannot be eradicated from any such program.

———

Of the many programs in existence at that time, ALE was one of the few, its clients were told, given its jurisdiction in New York State, that required clients to clean themselves weekly with more than a rag. Showers were such a rare perk that ALE became known as an easy program, one for the fainthearted.

Indeed, the activities at ALE and other wilderness programs seem harmless on paper, if monotonous. The only variance from one day to the next is the coming and going of other clients and the weather, with the daily routine of eat, hike, rest, eat, hike, rest, therapy, and sleep unchanged. After breakfast each morning, tents are torn down, followed by the packing of all personal items into a rucksack. Each aimless day is filled with hikes in no particular direction along with impromptu therapy sessions and timed pack drills requiring clients to empty and repack their bags. These drills make the clients—sometimes suffering from drug or alcohol withdrawal—sweat, and often mental or psychiatric breakdowns can occur.

Physical suffering and even death are nothing new when it comes to adventure education and wilderness programs. Shortly after the founding of many university-linked programs, a twelve-year-old boy died after suffering heatstroke at a similar program at Idaho State University. In 1975, a young woman died at BYU while traversing the Burr Desert in Utah. She had fallen to dehydration. Many instructors believed themselves to be doing "God's work," which meant that logistics and safety considerations, along with the requisite training, were hardly required or employed by staff.

Olsen revamped the program at BYU and updated the safety protocols, but roughly a decade later a thirteen-year-old plunged to his death in Idaho at a wilderness survival program, while for the next few decades an Arizona-based program would hold the record of reporting sixteen accidental deaths. By this time, the mideighties and early nineties, the programs had begun gearing themselves toward troubled teens. Two more deaths occurred: a teenage boy in Utah, whose autopsy revealed acute peritonitis from a perforated ulcer, an invasive infection reaching into his abdominal cavity (according to a report in *Outside* magazine, after being strip searched and issued boots and a hiking backpack, he was thrust into the wilderness, much like Hazel, and wrote in one of his first journals, "I've been shaking from the cold since I got here. My body being used to the weather in Phoenix is going into shock. I feel like I'm going to die . . . I am scared. I don't know when I can talk or if I can."); and a teenage girl who died at another wilderness program in Utah.

After these incidents, some speculation arose about the inherent dangers of such programs and the lack of oversight. It was then that the state of Utah enacted restrictions for outdoor corrective programs, instituting an 1,800-calorie minimum per day and weight restrictions for hiking packs. New York State and others would follow, after which clients at ALE showered once a week and consumed a certain number of calories daily, goals that most programs reportedly never enforced. The intake process was never scrutinized and remained the same for most clients; they arrived at the programs after being taken by transporters, known as escorts, who came to them one night and plucked them from the life they'd known. Everyone was stripped and searched and reduced to their most primitive selves.

Aspen Education Group, which oversaw ALE, had for years found itself roiled by abuse allegations and lawsuits, patient deaths and suicide.

Then in 2004, fourteen-year-old Matthew Meyer, a client at one of Aspen's wilderness programs, called Lone Star Expeditions, died from heatstroke after hiking for several hours. It took years for the school to settle the wrongful-death lawsuit, and further documentation about the program was sealed by the court. Reporting on the conditions of these programs and their clients proves difficult for anyone who either does not work in a program or has not been admitted to one: parents are just as cagey about their involvement as the private companies are about their treatment methods. When the programs were open about letting journalists or media behind closed doors, the portraits in those early years were often glowing. Shortly after Meyer's death, *Dateline* ran a piece extolling the effects Lone Star had on rebellious clients who "returned [home] a month later with a new outlook on life." But that outlook was never fundamentally good.

After an investigation in 2007 (with subsequent reports released in 2008), during the same time that Hazel wended through the first of two stints in wilderness therapy, the US Government Accountability Office noted ten deaths attributed to wilderness programs between 1990 and 2004. The report "found thousands of allegations of abuse, some of which involved death, at residential treatment programs across the country." Another estimate placed the "highest unconfirmed [death] count" of children in wilderness programs at eighty-six since 2000. Other criticism centered on the breaking of trust between parent and child due to the disingenuous way children were admitted to the wilderness programs. Yet the industry has continued to go generally unregulated.

Meanwhile, much of the research about wilderness therapy and its purported benefits has been conducted and funded internally. Over the past couple decades, to supplement the industry's own research, there has been a wealth of academic research into outdoor therapy. One study reinforced the understanding, based in part on outside studies, that wilderness therapy programs are generally effective. Some studies, either with smaller data pools or concerning participants with unique psychological issues, found programs to be detrimental. Still, several studies found that wilderness therapy programs could be beneficial and could provide lasting developmental growth to the participants if they were given sufficient aftercare. Other studies have focused on instructor and therapist training to "recognize and manage suicide risk and self-harm" and to engage in therapeutic activities addressing gender-specific trauma.

Today, there are some five thousand teenagers admitted to wilderness programs each year. When mentioning the Government Accountability Office report from 2007, proponents of wilderness therapy say that was in the past, despite the programs having changed very little since those Wild West days. What is missing are studies into the effects of forceful placement into wilderness therapy and the lasting effects of treatment conducted at residential treatment centers, which are often prescribed as a follow-up to wilderness therapy.

Michael Gass, a professor in the Outdoor Education Program at the University of New Hampshire, conducts the majority of wilderness therapy studies funded in part by the Outdoor Behavioral Healthcare Council, a nongovernmental accrediting body for the industry, and the National Association of Therapeutic Schools and Programs (NATSAP). Much of Gass's work is based around four questions: Is wilderness therapy safe? How does someone tell the difference between a good and a bad program? Is it worth the money? Moreover, does it work?

Gass and his researchers have worked over several decades to push the industry to a normative acceptance. To that end, he hopes that their work will validate the programs not only in the public sphere but also in the medical sphere, where they are constantly fighting for medical insurance providers to recognize and cover the programs.

"I think it's an evolutionary process," Gass told me. "I think insurance companies are just being careful. It's a financial issue."

Between 2014 and 2018, families began suing their health insurance providers for not covering such programs. Many insurers are not convinced that the treatments are anything more than experimental or that there is any conclusive evidence of their benefit.

"I wish we could be more certain on what we do, but that will take more time and effort," Gass said. As for the techniques used to get clients into the programs, like escorting and transporting, Gass added, "We need to address that."

3

If it had been quick and easy, what really would have been accomplished . . . ? The progress through the program depends a lot on your willingness to participate.

—Grandpa, excerpt from letter to Hazel

L et's all go around and say one thing we're thankful for," an instructor named Eddy said to Hazel and the other girls gathered around a campfire on her first full morning at ALE. He was good willed and meant well. He had the rough-hewn appearance of someone who had spent his life alone in a New England cabin, away from children. Small and rotund, he moved around the girls like a jungle cat, with his hiking pack flapping around his back. He believed he knew what could set them free, but he had no formal training, only manuals, guidebooks written by the program's director, and a short introductory course about which Hazel would learn only later.

"Alcohol," offered one girl.

"No, you can't say that," Eddy said.

"The sun?" said another.

"Good," Eddy replied.

"That it didn't rain last night."

"Good, great, that's really great stuff. Now let's take a personal inventory. How's everyone feeling? We can start over there, with Hazel."

"Tired," Hazel said, avoiding eye contact.

"Okay, tired's fine, I'm sure we're all a bit tired. But, how are you feeling?"

"Pissed."

"Good, good. Pissed is good. That's an emotion. It's important to be in touch with your feelings. Let's try and decipher why you're pissed."

"Because my grandma kidnapped me and brought me to the fucking middle of fucking nowhere."

This exercise carried through lunch. The group talked about how they felt their experience was going, what they missed, and what they anticipated from this journey, all while scribbling about past wrongdoings in large marbled notebooks.

Later that day the girls huddled over a fecal arrangement, folded into itself like soft-serve ice cream and dropped along a hiking path where the group had settled overnight. It was human, to be sure. Looked human, smelled human. The instructor took off his hat and ran a hand caked in mud through his hair.

"What have we said about leaving no trace, no evidence of us coming around here and setting up camp?" he began. "What have we said about the importance—no, not the importance, but the *necessity*—to keep this place clean and spotless for others to enjoy?"

He wanted someone to own this act of defiance. "Who made this surface poo?" he said. No one but him kept a straight face. The girls surveyed the ground, sometimes made eyes at one another. One of the girls turned to another and said, "Libby, you just went to the bathroom!" The girls knew that anytime someone left the group they had to ask for permission, and still, from afar, while squatting to relieve oneself, they had to shout their assigned number—"four, four, four!"—lest they tried to make an escape when out of view.

"I didn't fucking do it," Libby shouted and reached for a nearby stick, which she bent until it snapped and the crackle tore through the trees. She jammed the stick into her own arm, piercing it in several places. The blood reached the ground before the instructors were able to restrain her. Hazel watched as Libby was tackled, wrapped in a tarp, tied down by the instructors, and taken from the group forever.

The next morning, Hazel and the other clients circled around the campfire and recited their "hopefuls" for the day, presenting the group with their goals and desires for the accomplishments they hoped to make through therapy that day. If these goals weren't met, they would not get spices for dinner. No salt and pepper to doctor the blanched rice.

Hazel hated having to "constructively" call people out for things they did wrong just to get spices at the end of the day, but she knew that to get to Bear Phase, she would need to play the game. If the kids were honest and constructively criticized enough of their fellow clients—using therapeutic language like "justification" and "rationalizing" and "blame shifting," which they learned from the instructors overseeing their group, Group A, and their group's therapist, Joanne—they would sometimes be allowed to roast their tortillas over a fire and have a hot lunch.

In her first private meeting with Joanne later that day, Hazel learned that she'd been casually diagnosed with post-traumatic stress disorder. "I think it's just assumed with all of what has happened to me, that I must be some crazy person . . . they put a, like, thirteen-year-old on prescription drugs," Hazel reflected years later. Everyone in the group had a litany of their own diagnosed or undiagnosed problems.

Everything felt like it had to be learned again—how to stay warm, how to feed and clothe herself, how to not be consumed by her anxiety. It took her a while to adjust, to introduce herself and make small talk, a quiet girl making sure she had accounted for her gear, asking for a new sleeping bag. The hardest part of eating breakfast was not following the meal with a cigarette or two.

As the day's hike began, Hazel looked inward, thinking about when her Impact Letter would come and what it might say. Hazel believed that her problems were the faults of parental figures gone haywire all her life. Her faults were a product of the way her grandparents had treated her: if only she had been able to stay with her mother. What most gnawed at Hazel were the rumors that Paula had driven to the house in Saranac Lake on Church Street, demanding the release of her child. Hazel swore she heard her voice. But, because Paula did not have custody, she went home defeated, her latest boyfriend in tow.

"Can we stop?" asked Talia, a new client from Switzerland. Her clothes, like the ones worn by the rest of them, were tattered and dirty.

"I think she's about to pass out; we need to stop," said Alyse, the only other girl Hazel could stand in the group. Alyse stood with arms akimbo and watched Talia hyperventilate. Alyse had the compassion of a mother, with the motivation of a drill sergeant. She wanted the instructors to take notice of a struggling client. Alyse also wanted to make sure Talia did not threaten the group's chances of having salt and pepper—a privilege—with their dinner.

The instructors did not listen. Afraid of getting lost and left behind in a vast and unfamiliar wilderness, needing to make their final destination before dark, the group staggered in tow as Talia keeled over and relieved herself of breakfast on a rock in the snow. "This is a mistake, this is not where I'm supposed to be," Talia yelled through the chunks.

The shared consequences for the clients affected the group dynamics. If someone had an issue, the entire group had that issue. If someone ate from their bear bag outside of designated mealtimes, the group would take turns carrying that one girl's bear bag as punishment, the extra weight an added strain during hikes and bushwhacking. The bear bags, hung together in tall trees on a single line of climbing rope during the spring, summer, and fall to deter bears and, on that same rope, about five feet off the ground in the winter to deter critters, were full of food rationed for each girl for one week. No sharing allowed. Food could never follow someone back to the tents. Isolating the problem was meant to strengthen the group around that failure, to bolster them to hold each other accountable. Instead, it often led to animosity, rather than affinity. "I don't agree with that type of stuff because kids can be really exclusive and cliquey," Hazel said later. "The weakest link gets pushed out, and in wilderness that happened a lot."

———

Hazel weathered long hikes waiting for her Impact Letter and information about her present and future life. Hours felt like days or weeks. Looking back on the last few days and those moments before she was taken to the wilderness program, while she hiked, Hazel imagined being reunited with Simon as that morning hike grew into an afternoon hike and the slope of the hill seemed to curl up straight into the sky. Hazel was soon struck by the notion that there was no hope for returning home, even if she was not like Libby. She did not want to stab herself unconscionably, and she did not wish anyone dead, not even herself. The instructors often told the girls that if they felt hopeless, it was not because of the program; they had brought the hopelessness upon themselves. The instructors were backed up by therapists, like Joanne, who met with the girls individually once a week. She had blonde hair and blue eyes, both matte, rustic from years spent in thornbushes and patchy forests with ungrateful children. (Joanne's favorite refrain was something like "hurt people hurt people.") It was not their parents or the wilderness that was making them miserable but, rather, an innate issue that they were there to figure out. No client knew the time, because to know the time would have been to focus their energy and attention away from themselves. They called it FI, for *future information*, which they were not privileged to know. FI was not limited to time but also applied to current events—what celebrities were doing or whether the nation was mourning—and to their own fates after the program. The girls were forced to look backward, even if looking backward hurt. Hazel wanted her Impact Letter if only to console her in the terrifying notion that she would be gone for more than twenty-eight days and that this adopted life of hiking and woodworking and therapy had replaced everything. As in Hazel's life back home, it seemed that every time she tried to impress someone who was supposed to be her champion, they failed her, like Grandma or the police who would not listen to her. In her previous session, Joanne had told Hazel they were still waiting on her Impact Letter but could reveal no more "future information."

Then it came. On the night of her third full day, the attention turned to Hazel, the group's newest and most vulnerable. Eddy asked everyone to be quiet.

"I have your letter here," he told Hazel softly, the fire and his head-lamp providing the only light. "We can read it whenever you're ready. I'll look over your shoulder to make sure you're not skipping anything and that you're reading it as your parents wrote it."

"Grandparents," Hazel corrected hatefully. It was pitch-dark outside.

"You can use my headlamp to read it."

Dear Hazel,

Here we are helping to write another chapter in your life. This one I think will have a happy ending. This letter sounds like one I wrote to you not that long ago—same old shopworn phrases, but you know what? They're still important to listen to.

It was not pleasant yesterday and I hope we will all get over it, because we "must move on" (a corny phrase, but how true).

Your grandma has outlined to you how your recent behavior is totally unacceptable (you know that I know all about it) and you are hurting and disappointing people around you. But what is more important is that you are hurting yourself. Nobody really wants to do that. The little lies here and others there, dabbling in drugs and alcohol have all added up to a very nasty situation. The relationship with Simon (Grandma would say addiction, and I agree) is too intense for you two. Neither of you knows yet who you are, and until that time, it will dominate your life at the expense of other things you could be doing. It has already led you back into drugs and alcohol. Your schoolwork is suffering and, tragically, you were dismissed from your performing activities, which is something that you really enjoyed and were very good at. I cannot begin to tell you how sorry I was for you about that happening. What a pity.

Much more of your life is ahead of you than behind. You have had a bumpy road through the early part of your life (those clichés keep coming, don't they, but stay with me here) and you lost out on some childhood. You remember about the "straight and narrow," about it being not that straight and not that narrow? You can take small detours. There is enough wiggle room to be everything you want to be and still keep on track. And it's really the safest and best place to be. You may think when I talk with you that I am making light of this, Hazel, but that's my style. As you know, words are my business and it is just a cheap trick to get your attention and to highlight the seriousness of what is out there . . .

When you were standing beside your mom yesterday, I saw how tall you have gotten. The word would be "rangy," not "gangly." I bet you could reach around and give yourself a hug. Why don't you put this letter down and do that right now.

It read like a soppy, misdirected letter of inspiration. Generally speaking, parents wrote in one letter as a unified body; Hazel's Impact Letter seemed to include the voice of her grandmother but only bore the signature of her grandfather. Her grandmother ended on a harsh note, saying that she needed to change or she would never be allowed back home and that, for the time being, Hazel was where she needed to be. Her grandfather was gentler and told her it was not a punishment.

"I remember it being raw. But after I heard some other stories, I realized I'm not that bad." The letters that the other girls read were different. One lit her sister's bed on fire while she was sleeping in it; another girl broke her mother's nose. "I just remember thinking, like, I'm around nothing but crazy. There were certain things I never knew about before I went to ALE but had started to learn from the other girls. If I had stayed home, maybe I wouldn't have been a teenager learning about what a deviated septum from cocaine was. It's a whole new world."

The only impact it had was silence on the group.

"How are you feeling?" Eddy asked, turning off his headlamp and returning the group to the flickering light of the fire.

"Fine," Hazel said. "I heard what they had to say."

Each girl in her group, seated in a circle around the fire, had spoken up to say one thing they had heard in the letter, reiterating Hazel's faults and reinforcing the notion that she was right where she belonged.

"It sounds like you're very loved and that you were a bit out of control," one girl said.

"It seems like the relationship with your mother is something to work on," another said.

It was strange to hear them comment on her life. Everything was exposed; she was no longer the new, enigmatic girl sitting in the corner quietly. As she turned in for sleep that night, she was thankful that the program seemed to now be getting underway, in the direction of home.

———

The next morning, Hazel was still lost to her thoughts of life back in New Jersey. Hiking now gave her time to think through the letter her grandparents had sent, the Impact Letter that she'd had to read in front of the group—a rite of passage for each girl, even if that rite was forced onto them and propelling them to Bear Phase.

The first few tasks of Bear Phase were simple. When Hazel was not hiking, she would spend time sharpening a large round stick, turning it over in her hands, roughing it into a spade with a sharp rock. The stick would be hers for digging latrines where she could "bust hundos," named for the distance from a water source a client must be before defecating. Though Simon and life back home remained her primary motivations to get out of the program, she slowly found herself learning the language of the program and becoming more focused on carrying out her tasks for her eventual move to Wolf Phase.

After completing the digging stick, she spent other hours making cordage, endless lengths of rope that she twined together. One day the girls sat in a tree-stump field called Elephant's Graveyard, splitting cedar bark, ripping free its brown threads, wetting the strands in a pool of water sanitized with chlorine tablets so that they could bite down on the knotted rope without fear of infection. Over and over she pulled taut the sinew, twisting as she imagined the inhabitants of this land had twisted years ago. To test its tensile strength, she would dangle a five-pound water bottle from the cord. For many weeks it would snap, sending her back to the beginning and further delaying her return home, to Simon.

The tasks kept coming and she kept failing: build a set of critter traps out of wood shingles and rock, or complete a ten-page narrative encompassing her life story, or fashion a walking stick out of a hard wood that could withstand being smashed against a tree by an instructor.

"Think this walking stick is ready?" Eddy asked one day.

"I hope so," Hazel said.

"You don't sound confident. Is that something we should explore?"

"No."

Eddy wound up, like a baseball hitter, and cracked the stick against a tree. It snapped in two. The days Hazel put into it were lost. She would have to start again.

Days became weeks. Hazel's group, the only one composed of girls, dwindled to only three. The group would fluctuate in size—reaching a maximum of nine—as girls graduated or were pulled by their parents. Hazel had been with the group when it was small; she was the third and last girl, after Libby was taken. Hazel was thankful her number would remain unchanged at three as new girls arrived, making her the third most senior girl in Group A. Unlike the other girls, she would not have to remember who had left and in what position she then was, an arbitrary ranking of seniority toward which the instructors urged their clients to strive.

Some hikes were far from their small wanderings around the tall pines and heavy hemlocks and spruce of upstate, though in which direction—toward the Tug Hill plateau, toward Canada—the group of girls never knew. "Stay focused on the here and now," an instructor called to the girls as they clambered into a black Ford Expedition with its windows tinted to match. Hazel stole a glance at herself in the side-view mirror. Her eyebrows had overgrown her face, and she stumbled back in shock. It was the first time she had seen herself in weeks, and the girl she saw in that mirror was not the girl she knew herself to be.

Hazel met with Joanne for their weekly therapy sessions, but as ever, the sessions carried on in an impersonal manner. Hazel, always excited to see Joanne (who held Hazel's only hope for FI and a connection to her world back home), met only a cold exterior. Even though Hazel had put in good effort to work through the program, it was impossible for her to evoke anything close to pride from Joanne. Besides, she was still only a Bear.

A ray of hope came two weeks later: inside the car on the way to their next expedition on a remote trail, a longer hike and journey far away from the therapists at base camp on the day when their bear bags were filled for the week ahead, she heard music for the first time since being taken. "Bury Me," by Thirty Seconds to Mars, and "Rehab," by Amy Winehouse, became their soundtrack as they drove along the serpentine mountain roads, the ballads of their young lives. Where the vehicle stopped, the snow had mixed with the swamps and the land caved into itself. They unloaded and started up the mountain hanging over them. The metaphor of reaching a summit despite the struggles toward the pinnacle was not lost on the girls, even as they fought against the elements and inadequate clothing.

"We'd go through swamps and get trench foot," Hazel said. "You're wearing loose-ass pants that are rubbing your thighs, which are wet. You're soaking wet. I remember the only time in my life when my thighs were bleeding and requesting Gold Bond for my legs. You had to walk with your pack off and walk straight through water. We were bushwhacking. So many times I was there and was, like, is this really allowed?"

She came to enjoy the hiking itself, which became a cathartic and rhythmic habit. On those arduous hikes up the mountain, the group, though mostly silent in their single-file line (Hazel sometimes sang Christina Aguilera songs to herself), bracketed by an instructor at the front and rear, challenged each other with riddles to pass the time. "There are fifty-two bicycles in a room and two dead men," one girl would shout back to the group. "What happened?" The inquiry would distract Hazel and the other girls, diverting them from the burning thighs and ankles, the thin air at the higher altitudes. If no one answered correctly (the men were playing poker), the riddle was traded for another.

Reaching the top was never easy, avoiding "fly back" branches as the girls cut their own trail, another metaphor never lost on the girls: it was important to be aware of the consequences for your actions. The small group came up with a jingle, sung to the tune of Fat Joe's "Lean Back": "Group A don't dance, we pull up our rain pants and push that branch away. Fly back, fly back."

The hiking never bothered Hazel. It mostly reminded her of Grandpa, her life back home. Long since divorced from Hazel's grandmother, but still a strong presence in the family, he fought against the degradation of Hazel's relationship with her grandmother, often acting as an unsolicited go-between and a de facto safe space. He had encouraged her throughout the car ride and in her Impact Letter to take advantage of the opportunities ALE would provide. He often found solace in the wilderness, the outdoors, long before that morning in the car with the granddaughter he no longer recognized, no longer knew, and no longer understood. He hiked all his childhood, all his life, summiting Mount Rainier in Washington State and Mount Shasta in California, and he often took Hazel on hikes and biking through mountain passes. They would trek through the cone-bearing eastern hemlocks of the Delaware Water Gap National Recreation Area, or they would fold themselves into cups of hot chocolate on frozen lakes in northern Maine or the Panther Lake campground in Byram Township in New Jersey, where families could rent cabins or trailers along the water's edge. At the Anthony's Nose peak along the Hudson River, in New York, Grandpa took Hazel and her brother deep into a wooded area. (When the two siblings were alone at the mountains, Hazel's brother clasped his hands behind his back as Hazel shared her most cherished secrets. "I pick my boogers and eat it!" "I like Jeremy Brennan!" Hazel did not know that her admission of the crush she had in first grade was not as secret as she believed, for her brother had pulled out from behind his back a Yak Bak voice recorder and played her secret on repeat.) When the three were not adventuring across a gorge or lake, Grandpa took the children twice a week for a meal at Taco Bell or McDonald's, like on the day they dropped Hazel off at Saranac Lake.

Over the next week, as nights grew colder and lonelier as the clients received the harsh winter, some of the most arduous tasks were not therapeutic but skill based, like making the walking and digging sticks. The critter traps always stumped Hazel. They always seemed to collapse when an instructor came by to test them, shaking the ground beneath their footfall. After she had strained for hours one day to set up three small traps, the last of her skills before she could request a transfer to Wolf Phase, she called to Eddy. She liked Eddy. Unlike the other instructors, he did not seem preoccupied with solitude in the wilderness but, rather, had a genuine interest in the girls and their well-being, although sometimes misdirected and untherapeutic, compared to Joanne. He was not always the brightest instructor, communicating through grunts and strong silences, and misspelling words in his notes to the clients when reviewing their daily journals, but he was kind.

"Are you sure these are ready? I don't want them to fall any more than you do," Eddy said.

"I hope they don't," Hazel said. "My trigger sticks are better this time, I think."

"All right, let's test your trap line."

Eddy stomped around on either side of the critter traps, constructed of twigs, cordage, and a heavy rock or log as the deadfall. The deadfalls shook a bit, but nothing was triggered and the traps held. Then he engaged each trigger, as though a mouse or small animal were pecking away at the food set out for them, and each trap collapsed as it should.

Eddy would have high-fived her, but it was against the rules. Instead, he sunk his hands into his pockets, smiled, and turned before walking away.

Most instructors seemed nearly interchangeable: all were in their late twenties or early thirties, carried the same Mountain Hardwear fanny pack, and seemed to understand at least the fundamentals of wilderness first aid. Some had trouble reading maps and using a compass, but most seemed to know the terrain well enough. Most were from the North Country, born and raised around the Adirondacks or having recently graduated from a college in New Hampshire where many majored in wilderness therapy. The education was not a qualifier for a therapy license; rather, like Outward Bound, it prepared its graduates for competency in the outdoor world and that was all.

Eddy, during a hike, began bleeding from his nose and ears and kept on hiking. "I mean, at that point, I was just like, *I guess no one's in good hands and no one knows what the fuck they are doing*, especially when Eddy was bleeding out of his ears the first night," Hazel said. "And some of the men, [the] men didn't know how to deal with the young women." As young girls, they were not sure they were protected. Even though they had for so long touted their individualism, they recognized then, more than ever, that there needed to be someone overseeing their safety.

Donna was an instructor most girls hated to have on their team. They knew when she arrived for her stints with them that their week would be tough and mismanaged. Donna seemed like she needed therapy of her own and made the girls hike twice as far or for twice as long. She made the girls do pack drills late into the night.

"We're going to keep doing this until everyone does it right, and on time," she said one night under a storm.

"But can't you see we're about to be hit by that storm?" a girl shouted.

"If you hurry up, it won't make a difference," Donna shouted back.

The girls went about pulling everything out of their bags, dumping everything onto the cold wet earth, then cramming everything back in under a minute. The exercise was exhausting, and because it had gotten so late, they missed dinner and were told to set up their tarps and go to sleep unfed.

Hazel was the quickest at pack drills and felt a growing distrust and hatred of the girls in her group because they were the reason she was not having dinner, a feeling not unique to anyone who was in the program long enough and had grown proficient, if not jaded. But these feelings were not the trait of a Wolf, Hazel knew, and before going off to bed, she offered to help one or two of the new girls work on their knots. She was growing to be the group's leader.

To be at this point, four weeks into her program near the beginning of December and heading into Wolf Phase, meant Hazel had "put forth considerable effort in fulfilling the objects of Bear Phase," according to the Growth Book. Hazel's book, now tattered and damp from weeks spent trekking through waist-high waters and steep inclines into the clouds, acted as much as a guide as the compass and map the instructors carried with them. "Now, you must take the next step and request a transition feedback group with your peers and instructors to request permission to move forward to Wolf Phase." Hazel was striving to make her grandparents proud, if only to convince them to bring her home. They exchanged a volley of letters every few days. And as the days slogged forward, the letters and small acts of human kindness made this new life in the woods her actual life, replacing whatever hopes and dreams she had for returning to New Jersey. It replaced the life she had before. Phases and hard skills and soft skills and journal entries were what mattered most. She could conceive of nothing more.

One of the rewards of Wolf Phase was the privilege of picking out your bear bag first on food-drop days: a chance to rummage through the bags to pick the one with the best block of cheese, the headiest pepperoni, though during hikes the clients traded rations behind the instructors' backs. Some people swapped brown sugar for peanut butter or tortillas for more cheese. If they were caught, they were met in the morning with cold oats that had not had the time to expand or saturate in hot water, making the meal akin to eating mortar, which felt to Hazel like abuse, stacked among the many other small deprivations.

When they huddled around the campfire at another rustic camp-site, Hazel requested feedback for transition to Wolf Phase. It was sup-posed to be a chance for her to listen to the others about things she could improve, but instead it was used as an open attack against her.

"We think you're a bit pretentious, honestly," said Adriana, one of the new girls. "We know you've been here for, like, almost two months but, honestly, we're all struggling, so I imagine you taking this tran-sitional period to reflect on your humility and role as a leader in this group."

Hazel hated Adriana. They sniped at each other, trading rude comments beneath their breath. They argued on the trail, tripped one another with each other's hiking sticks. Because of this last incident and how it could have seriously injured them or another client, they were made to use a bow drill in tandem earlier in the day as a way of settling their differences. The bow drill, used to create a fire through a turning rod against a piece of pine or hemlock, was a metaphor for their power struggle. Adriana had come back for a second stint in wilderness, from some other program, and seemed more knowledgeable about the system in which the girls found themselves. She moved between hope-fuls and thankfuls seamlessly and, like Hazel, spoke the language of the instructors. Hazel had all but memorized her Growth Book, internal-izing nothing but memorizing everything. At this moment, though, she focused on Adriana's facial hair, the way her offset jaw revealed her yellowed canines.

"I want to second that," another girl chimed in. "Your constructive feedback to others in the group always seems a bit like it is meant to harm or hurt. It's like you hate us, and we don't know why."

"I hear what you are saying," Hazel said at the end of her feedback group. "And I am thankful. I know that the word humility comes from *humilis*, which means 'of the earth,' like it says in our Growth Book, and so I want to go into this next phase, my Mask of Black, with an idea of returning to my roots, to returning to my earth mother and internalizing the feedback I've received tonight."

This seemed to please the instructors because, before everyone crawled beneath their tarps for another night beneath the stars, one of the instructors came to Hazel and pulled her away from the group. She was being taken on a "solo," which signaled her transition from Bear to Wolf. "The solo was called Mask of Black, and you had to stay away from the group for two days," Hazel explained. "You can have your own personal fire, which I thought was cool. But you couldn't talk to anyone, and that was my worst nightmare."

From outside the group, Hazel began to view her place among this tribe of young women with introspection. "We were all put through the same wringer—solidarity—going through the same bullshit together," she said. "It's like you went to war with someone. I hated a lot of those girls, but in some ways, I loved them because everything was out there in the open; there was nowhere to hide, nowhere to not share something, to sugarcoat your life." Without consent, she had joined this group and invested in the people, other than herself. In this way, the program was beginning to work. She was thinking beyond herself.

In her final weeks at ALE, near the end of December, Hazel made a new friend. The girl, Kelsey, was new to the group, but Hazel and she clicked. They shared a similar demeanor—that of the carefree girl with a chip on her shoulder, though perhaps those traits beget one another. During one of Kelsey's first nights, when she read her own Impact Letter to the group, Hazel loved the way Kelsey rolled her eyes at every sentence, mocking her parents from afar. It was a slight but not insignificant victory. Hazel felt that Kelsey, too, did not need to be there, and soon they sat hip to hip at every meal. When someone they did not like was talking, they would nudge each other. "It was the only time we could touch," Hazel said. Sometimes they passed notes. Before an instructor could catch them, they would toss the correspondence into the fire. For the first time in years, Hazel was sober and experiencing relationships organically. She felt human in the shared space. These feelings of settlement abated often. In their place came the fear surrounding an ever-expanding universe of uncertainty. As Hazel compared herself to others, she watched as different paths into the future revealed themselves.

Hazel was vying to graduate from Wolf Phase to Hawk Phase when Kelsey's parents decided to pull her out after a few weeks into her program. She would not have to sit in the mud any longer. She would not have to make a bow-drill set out of hemlock. She could toss her Growth Book into the fire and never think again of the wilderness therapy program. It was a blessing and a damnation, however, because she would not be going home to the family she left; her mom had been diagnosed with cancer. To Hazel, this made sense: nothing good in Hazel's life could stay, even if she felt some sorrow for Kelsey. Amid all her selfishness, Hazel grappled with a shred of empathy.

The final months of wilderness are akin to a climber ascending a mountain. Having faced challenges of both mental and physical stress, the climber reaches a figurative summit of achievement and is required to "descend" from this summit without losing any gains that resulted from her achievements. Rushing through this descent could very well result in regression, erasing all the good achieved on the hike and endangering the climber. The post-wilderness client, or more accurately the parents of the client in treatment, was urged to consider extra treatment after wilderness therapy, continuing a separation from their home life (which may be the source of their negative lifestyle), and developing a long-term support system (through the family and their new holistic relationships) to reintegrate to regular home life.

There was nothing any client could control about their future or the way their program changed their eventual placement in other programs to further their therapy. "The loss of control is just what's scarier than everything," Hazel said. The point of these programs is to break you. And Hazel felt broken. "That's my biggest problem with wilderness," she said. "No future information. You can't know what time it is. That's the scariest . . . just to take away everything. Like I said about the hair ties, taking away my black hair tie, giving me an identical one that was theirs just so I had nothing that was me. Stripped completely of yourself. And for a kid that's not okay."

———

Wilderness therapy is effective only in the short term, many industry skeptics believe, though Hazel would never know whether or not she would have been fine to return home. The thinking goes that to transition into deeper, long-term therapy is to advance a client's therapeutic needs, allowing for the recognition and processing of mental and emotional issues in a more real-world environment. The intended goal—of reintegrating the client through further intensive treatments—only acts to cleave them farther from the world.

In many studies, clients have indicated that wilderness therapy was productive for them during and immediately after it and the rest of their treatment. Interviews have shown that the clients usually did not continue to develop in the years after wilderness treatment, aside from the usual maturation of the adolescent brain and personality. Because a patient is swiftly reintroduced to their old peer groups, they shed any skills learned while in therapy. The transition is abrupt, and the tools learned in wilderness are lost outside of a controlled environment. Yet the experience does not derail them socially, which may be the best benefit to a swift return.

Instead, wilderness treatment is more than a transitional phase from the real world. The wilderness experience is a small and underwhelming way to inculcate clients in the language and expectations of therapy. It prepares them for the larger residential institutions into which they are forced later, even if every client's parents do not decide on that route for their child (though many of them are often heavily encouraged to take this route). And the inoculation does not always disturb a child's otherwise normal tendencies. Sustained treatment through aftercare is essential to the pipeline of these programs, and the transition from intense wilderness therapy to more-targeted and long-term residential programs is always directed.

Hazel had become resigned to this fate, a fate she had only learned about after Adriana entered the group from a different program. Hazel knew that, even when she left, she likely would not be returning to the home or the life that she had known.

On Christmas Eve, Hazel and the group of girls had neared the summit of a tall regional peak. "The snow was cool. It was snow, just snow, and it was pitch-blue sky, and we were basically inside a pine forest on the top of a mountain," Hazel said years later. "It was the most beautiful thing."

This memory would remain. Many others would not. Wilderness was like that, wilting in her recollection as she focused her attention forward, the days of hiking and sumping and being hopeful and thankful receding into an inaccessible bloc inside her. Those moments in wilderness were her past now. Simon and her mother seemed forever away, as though they were dreams. Her school friends and past life were gone. She was trying to accept that the only way to get those back was to look forward, where her life remained out of her control, something she would knuckle through.

She sat at the mountain's edge. The world stretched before her seemed so clear, even across the jagged landscape and its hazy gradation toward the horizon. Before her was a carpet unlike anything she had ever seen: mountains and rolling hills cascading into the distance. She had never felt so complete; even if the path before her was less than clear, she could see for miles.

The hike down hurt her knees. She grabbed hold of small twigs that snagged bits of her skin and tore at her clothing as she navigated the trail. She was ahead of Talia, who almost collapsed into her, having slipped on a wet rock. Both had left their hiking sticks down at base camp, an attempt to shed weight but also prove that they did not need the crutch.

When they reached the campfire, the group fell onto their packs and sighed at the sky. Descending was easier, yes, but the packs burdened them, and they knew that soon they would set about doing some therapeutic task, like setting up critter traps together, or another truth circle, or maybe the new girl would have her Impact Letter ceremony. They would never know: nearly everything they wanted to know was FI. Hazel laughed. It was Christmas, and she was in the woods worried about whether she might get salt and pepper to eat with her lentils later. *What a life,* she thought.

The instructors returned from a huddle and handed each client Christmas gifts. "They made us Kellogg's Rice Krispies Treats with M&M's, and we were on a sugar high for real," Hazel said. "We got a disposable camera, knitting needles—it was a really fun night. Santa came."

The next morning Hazel followed an instructor down a path. The path was like a wet scar in the earth, the only brown through a blanket of snow. At the end of the path, Hazel saw her grandma, grandpa, brother, and mother stumbling through the forest.

She had heard the shrieks and yelps from moments like this before, for other girls as they reunited with family, and had always imagined it a silly reunion: how could anyone be happy to see the same people who had initiated the incarceration? Yet she began to cry and bounded toward her mother. It was her fiftieth day in the woods.

Hazel said goodbye to her group and scrambled into the family's rented minivan. The departure was quick and cold, a heartless decoupling that felt surreal. The moment she had wanted for weeks had finally come and, just as quickly, was now over. Immediately, she began to forget the group, Eddy, Joanne, and Donna and focused her attention ahead and to things she could not while at ALE: she could worry herself about the future and forget herself in the present. Inside the minivan, Hazel glanced in the mirror to see how wiry her eyebrows had become, to remember again what she looked like, but became all the more elated by something else. She saw a clock on the dashboard and shouted, "I know the time! It's eleven a.m.!"

The family had heard that Hazel would take some time to readjust. They drove the minivan out of the woods with the windows down, to air out the car. "Everyone just groaned, and they rolled down the windows because I smelled so bad. I had permanent dirt on all my knuckles. When I sat in a bath later, it was brown, immediately brown water." For a week afterward, her hair smelled of campfire.

On their way out of Saranac Lake, Hazel and her family passed the McDonald's they had first visited less than two months before. As they drove, she watched the world pass by through the windows of the minivan as she listened to Christina Aguilera and the other artists she had missed for all those weeks away. Something else dawned on her, something she had turned over in her mind ever since those first nights in the wilderness: no matter where she was, everything continued on with or without her, making her feel small, which made her think of drugs and the way they righted everything that felt wrong. She wanted pot and started scheming for a way to get some, but she gave up as she glanced at the door handles and knew they were locked.

Hazel changed the moment she left wilderness, back to her former self. She dialed Simon from the hotel where her family had stopped for the night.

"Where have you been?" he said, the line staticky.

"In the strangest program, in the strangest place, you wouldn't believe it," Hazel said. "Everything was crazy."

"It sounds it."

"Yeah."

Silence.

"Well, how are you?" Hazel said.

"I'm good, but busy," Simon said. "I've got to get going here in a minute."

"Oh," Hazel said, self-consciously and nearly ashamed. "Well, they're taking me somewhere else now. I can call you before then, maybe?"

"Yeah, I don't know if I'll be around," Simon said and hung up.

Hazel felt betrayed, focused on everything she could not control, the rubrics of wilderness therapy slipping away: the therapeutic lessons had little application in the real world, no influence over Simon's world, the outside world, that world she once called home.

BOOK II

Residential

Avery

1

I have personally noticed the lack of effort in school, extracurricular activities, interactions with your siblings, and completion of the minimal chores we have requested at home. While I see you stay up late, it was generally not to study or to improve yourself, rather it was to talk on the phone as much as possible, as late as possible, and with disregard to your schoolwork . . . Your overall affect, facial expressions and behavioral makeup, have been bland, sad, or minimal recently.

—*Avery's godmother, excerpt from Impact Letter to Avery*

The drive up the mountain to the Academy at Swift River had immobilized Avery, stunning her as though the shock treatment she imagined awaited at her destination. Her godmother had duped her into coming after completing a stint in wilderness therapy, the gateway to other—sometimes stricter—types of therapy. Only after a student or client rediscovered himself or herself in a natural environment, revitalizing their human spirit and encouraging the mending of broken emotional bones, could they accept further treatment. Or so the thinking goes.

Huddled in the foothills of the Berkshire Mountains of Massachusetts, the Academy at Swift River was a college preparatory school surrounded by over six hundred acres of mixed forest, meadows, beaver ponds, mountain streams, and marked trails. An octagonal cupola towered above the main house, a long white-and-green clapboard building. More white buildings were scattered about lush fields, the campus dotted with plum trees and lavender blossoms and black-eyed Susans. The closest some clients, or in this program those considered students, might get to the Ivy League was Swift River's tuition, nearly double the cost of a year studying at Harvard. Inside the clapboard buildings, along the hallways, were photo collages of current and past students, smiling, content, rock climbing, or posing along a stream in western Massachusetts.

The photos belied what experience lay ahead for Avery.

———

Before she transferred from wilderness therapy to the residential treatment center called Academy at Swift River, Avery never found the stability associated with home. Her idea of home was something rickety. Avery was born in Boston in the summer of 1991. She was raised by her biological mother, who, like Hazel's mother, was addicted to drugs and struggled with alcohol. Avery's sister, who was thirteen years old when Avery was born, ran away to live with her dad in Tennessee, leaving Avery alone with her mother in a trap house in the Boston neighborhood of Dorchester. "Then it was just me and my mom," Avery said. "Before I began talking, my mother would let men do things to me for drugs."

She would spend three years with her mother, traveling across New England, assaulted by her mother's boyfriends or the loitering relative. One day in New Hampshire, her mother was shooting heroin and passed out in the driver's seat of their Chevrolet, with Avery in the back seat. Her mother was arrested shortly after. Avery's godparents got custody of her and moved her to Louisiana.

Officially adopted and living now in a state far from New England, Avery seemed headed for a more stable life. She moved into a small house with a yellow room she called her own. But her new situation proved just as fraught as before. She had never been comfortable around men, sweating when they came too close to her. Her godmother's husband had a relative who lived in the shingle-clad house with them. At night, when everyone including Avery was asleep, he would stalk into her room. Sometimes, when her godmother and godfather were at work, the "uncle" would escort her into his room, leaving the door slightly ajar, unafraid anyone might disturb them. "I didn't want to tell my godmother," Avery said later. "I was trying to protect her; she had already taken me out of a bad situation, and I couldn't imagine how her knowing about what was happening in her house was going to make her feel."

Avery began acting out. When she was nine, the relative was kicked out of the house, not for his abuse but because he was dead weight—financially, emotionally—acting against the family. Even with him gone, Avery could hardly sleep, kept awake by the worry he might somehow get back into the house. Her panic became insomnia and a worsening affliction. She struggled to find ways to fall asleep on her own. Easy solutions were hard to come by.

Four years later she started dating a boy named James, her first real relationship, something she had sought on her own. Her godmother set boundaries, telling Avery that she was not allowed to speak with James after a certain hour at night and prying into her social life to discern whether James would be at a friend's house for a visit Avery said was just an outing with the girls. He lived next door and was close enough, but her godmother monitored their movements, Avery's relationship, with a watchful eye.

Fights with her godmother became more frequent, and after a particularly bad one, she ran to her room and slammed the door shut behind her. She grabbed a compact disc and cracked it in half, then ran the sharpest edge down her forearm. It was something she learned from a television show she had watched when she was younger, quickly becoming the solution she needed to combat her internal afflictions. Self-harm is commonly mythologized as attention-seeking behavior. It is not. The physicality of self-harm is meant to fill a void. When a person is unable to discuss with someone, to release their anxiety or depression or low self-esteem, they find avenues through their own body. Sometimes this manifests in sexual deviance or violence. Others bring the violence to themselves. When an injured person is in pain, the body releases endorphins and endocannabinoids, which is what Avery was after. The release was everything she sought. Time and life were things easily managed. All she needed was pain.

Avery loved James, though they never had sex or even kissed, which may have been what angered her most: they were responsible through abstinence (unlike some of her peers), but her godmother made her feel like a criminal. A lack of trust dissolved her relationships, including, eventually, with James. Not long after they made their relationship official with friends, James cheated on her with Avery's best friend and they broke up. Avery had again become distrustful of men and their intentions. Even the ones who pledged their love were lying. It made her all the more desirous of—she might say *delirious for*—their attention, their bodies. So she put time and effort into making herself look good for them, dolling herself up and making sure she looked enticing. She wanted someone to find her worthwhile. It was a desire inspired by force and a childhood of sexual admonishment. The first time Avery learned of sex, it was as something used to keep her silent. Ever since, for much of her adolescence, she was itinerant, her mind adrift from a body that was never quite her own.

This sense of foreboding followed her into a private Christian high school in Covington, Louisiana. No matter into what school or environment she was placed, her ability to connect with the other students had deteriorated. She emotionally pushed herself farther to the fringe of the school's social ecology but still wanted to try something to find a connection to her peers, to make good on the attention she was seeking. So she decided to try out for the cheerleading squad.

"The squad is really small, and since you can tumble, you have experience, you'll be fine," one of the cheerleaders said to her in the locker room before heading into the gym for the tryout. Laney, a thin blonde girl who was captain of the squad, came out onto the gymnasium floor and immediately shot a rude glance toward Avery. She felt alone beneath Laney's glare, self-conscious about her appearance. Avery was pretty, with big eyes and a delicate nose. Her chin stuck out proudly and pointedly, and she knew that her chest was one of her biggest assets. But she had a waistline that seemed unfit for cheerleading, something she hoped her other attributes might overshadow. She also imagined that being the only black girl was working against her.

After practice, Laney took Avery back to the lockers and had her kneel in front of a toilet. "You need to start throwing up after you eat," she said. "You're not skinny enough to be a cheerleader." She stood behind Avery until she puked. "You're the fat black girl, I guess," Laney added.

Following their captain's lead, the squad began to target Avery for ridicule and practical jokes. The girls would hide Avery's uniform before practice, hide her bloomers and her socks and her underwear. In retaliation, Avery stole Laney's cell phone and started making prank phone calls. When she returned the phone, Laney never knew, but another girl on the squad did and reported her. The school expelled her for violating school policy, which had a bylaw against theft and lying.

"It wasn't a big ordeal at school," Avery said. "It was a big ordeal at home."

For months before the expulsion, Avery had told her godparents about the girls mistreating her and how they made her feel, and she finally came clean about her uncle and the abuse suffered at his hand. "I don't know if they didn't believe me or didn't care," Avery said.

"You just need to deal with it," she recalled her godfather saying.

When "dealing with it" did not work, Avery's behavior grew more troubling, and her godparents decided to deal with the problem by sending her away, making her a problem that was no longer theirs.

Avery was first lured to Lone Star Expeditions, a wilderness therapy program, for a total of sixty days. Her godmother promised a shopping spree that then turned out to be a hook and Avery the sucker.

"At that point, by the time that you go to wilderness, you know that your childhood is over, your life is completely different," Avery said years later. "You are not a normal person. I mean, I don't think I ever felt normal . . . Leaving all of my friends, going to a school all year around, and having such stringent therapy? That's not normal."

Her wilderness therapy program seemed to placate her. Nothing was getting better, only duller. After her two months at the Lone Star wilderness program in Texas (where fourteen-year-old Matthew Meyer had died), Swift River was different, but not better.

"I thought Swift River was the strangest thing under the sun," Avery said as she recounted her first day. "I thought it was child abuse, honestly. What the hell is this and where the hell am I? What do you mean I can't leave? What do you mean I can't sign myself out until I'm eighteen? I'm going to graduate, without going home, from a boarding school that's year-round?"

Having been through rigorous weeks of wilderness therapy and hiking, Avery was leery of anything calling itself "therapeutic." On that first day at Swift River, standing in the alcove of the main building, off a main corridor where both boys and girls casually strolled as silhouettes against windows laced with thin black wires, which, if tripped, would send the school into lockdown, Avery felt alienated instantly.

The people there, like the short girl who greeted her just beyond the front doors, were not like her. Avery was black, and most of them were not. Some were dark skinned, but Avery felt the passing glare of students who tried to glimpse the new girl. The other girls stared at Avery and snickered, whispered about the makeup and the clothing with the brand names splashed on Avery's hips and across her chest.

The girl who had greeted her was not one of the gawkers. A spritely blonde, she had arrived at Avery's side and glanced up at the new arrival, her chin nearly resting on Avery's shoulder. "I'm Brie," she said and smiled pearly white. Her skin was strikingly pale, as if she had deliberately hidden from the sun all her life. She handed Avery a cold soda bottle. "They used to give us cans for these tours, but then they worried students would cut their wrists with the tabs," Brie said. "Are you a cutter?"

"Yes," Avery said, used to the curt and irreverent introduction from her time in the wilderness program.

"Well, then, here's your bottle and thanks for ruining cans for us." Brie smiled and waited for one back, but it never came. Recovering, Brie said, "I'm an ambassador for new students. Seriously, enjoy the soda, because this is just a first-day treat for anyone who isn't an ambassador. Sugar and soda are major no-no's here." But Avery did not react to her and instead looked past Brie, out the two doors at the far end of the alcove. Beyond the doors were a courtyard and a chicken coop, without chickens, painted to match the other buildings, white with green trim.

"I'll show you around, and I get to tell you where everything is, which is great, because that means I don't have to go to class today. We'll get to see everything, and your mom can chat with Frank and Tanya, the heads of the school." She kept saying "school," but Avery knew it was not so easy to define.

She followed Brie down a hall. Small clusters of students scrambled as Avery and Brie walked the hall toward the dining room. Lunch was nearly done. Plates were put into big black bins atop a conveyor belt, which fed into the kitchen and a heavy cloud of steam. Dispensers of milk stood at the end of several food containers against the far wall. Avery caught a hint of butter and hand sanitizer hanging in the air.

"We eat every meal here," Brie said. "I love the eggs, but others say they taste like rubber. I like breakfast, any breakfast really. Breakfast is like home, no matter where you have it." Avery liked eggs, too, but said nothing.

Students streamed out of the room, tucking chairs beneath the many wooden tables as they made their way through a series of doors behind Avery, out into another courtyard, and up a long trail that disappeared into a school building along the farthest ridge.

They turned past the double doors, which led down a hall past a long wooden staircase ascending to a second story. Avery paused and Brie said, "We do all of our meetings up there, and sometimes we hang out there just for fun. That's where we do things when we're not in school." Avery followed Brie up the stairs, and as they alighted onto the last step, Avery looked out across the vast space. "We call this the Great Room," Brie said.

It was the hayloft of what once was a barn. The ceiling reached several stories high, gabled and stretched by tough wooden beams. A miniature stage sat at the far end of the room, and green fabric couches spread into a semicircle facing the stage. The windows were fashioned into quarters by small strips of wood framing. There was a porch beyond locked doors, and near the top of the stairs was an office with a sign that read "Staff Only." Brie watched Avery without taking in the room, which she had come to know well since first arriving many months before. "Are you okay? I know this is a really hard day."

"I'm fine," Avery said and followed Brie back down the stairs, out the double doors, and toward a small cottage at the edge of the courtyard.

"There used to be a swimming pool here," Brie said, pointing to shards of wood and loam mixed with mulch. "But someone tried to drown another student, so they filled it with cement and, voilà, garden thing."

The cottage was the dormitory for the girls. Brie grabbed Avery's hand and pulled her into her room. She showed Avery around the space, then led her into the bathroom.

"Where is everything?"

"Everything? Oh, you mean the makeup? Well, we're not allowed makeup, and that Bebe shirt you're wearing—they're going to take that from you," Brie said. "It's about equalizing everyone, except the staff can wear makeup and straighten their hair."

"We can't straighten our hair?"

"Yeah, it's rough," Brie said. "Like prison!"

Avery's appearance was everything to her. The way she looked was the foundation of her own self-acceptance. Without razors, too, she felt that her hair would become unmanageable, that boys would hate her, that no one would see who she really was.

Brie walked back into the common area of the dorms, near where they had entered, and led Avery out again through the courtyard. The two walked in silence through the summer heat. A breeze unfurled off the pond as they passed. A frog hopped from a lily and plunged into the water.

"We have to walk super slowly," Brie said. She had no watch (Avery knew this meant FI was limited here, as it had been in wilderness) and was trying to time her late arrival by interpreting the sun. She was hoping to miss the rest of her science class.

"How long are we here for?" Avery asked as they reached the school.

"We are here for however long our parents and Frank and Tanya decide," Brie said, speaking of the program's directors. "The average program length is, like, eighteen months." Avery started to cry.

"It could be shorter! You have to work hard, though . . . don't cry," Brie said. "Well, at least you don't have to worry about mascara running. And at least the classes are co-ed. There are some real cuties here."

Avery choked out a laugh, but still she was scared. Eighteen months seemed an eternity to be away from home, from the familiar surroundings and her friends. She had yet to understand that the length of the program was not some number on a page but, rather, a prescription, a guidebook, that would determine how she got home rather than when. Though most students were there for eighteen months, lengths of stay varied. Some students only stayed a semester, roughly six months. Others had been known to stay for up to twenty-four months, through to completing their high school diploma. Those months were interspersed with intensive—group and individual—therapy sessions, merits and activities that could lead to someone completing their program faster, or disciplinary actions that could hold a student back. A student's program length was determined by clinical problems and the assessments given in wilderness therapy. The real challenge for each student was navigating the therapy and program through a series of tiered levels, which granted or revoked privileges and advancement through Swift River's school. The first few weeks were called Pathways. Avery would wear a uniform (green polo, khaki pants), the same as the other students in Pathways, and was subjected to team-building exercises (trust falls, ropes courses) and bonding activities (scavenger hunts, night hikes) as they acclimated to the program and its system of levels. It felt like the phases of wilderness all over again. Complete the requisite therapy and show growth and a student could move through Pathways to Levels One through Four to make their way home more quickly.

Moving through those levels, as Brie explained on their way up to the schoolhouse, was difficult. It required being honest and vulnerable. Each student was assigned a therapist who ran a group session with their team of students and with whom a student met weekly. In those individual and group meetings, students focused on repairing their relationships with their parents, talking freely about grappling with addiction, and discussed coping methods for their ailments. But treatment never stopped there. Teachers, counselors, therapists, and even the kitchen and nursing staffs all kept a close eye on students' behavior.

Swift River had its own language and consequences. All students signed a contract upon enrollment, stating that they would not physically harm themselves or others, they would not do drugs or drink alcohol, and they would not engage in sexual activities. Reprimands, for violating these "agreements" or misbehaving or disrespecting their parents, were handed down at all hours, even if therapists or counselors were not around. Progressively worse punishment came to those who continued breaking rules. If two students were seen holding hands, they might be placed on "bans," during which time they were forbidden from talking to that student. If they were again seen touching, they could be put on a "self-study," during which time they could speak only to students in their therapy groups and were made to sit alone at meals, writing in notebooks about what they did wrong and why they would not do it again.

"Challenges" were more individual and lonesome than "self-studies" and were reserved for students who brought drugs into school, abused their medications, or had sexual interactions with another student. These students were sent into total isolation and received no privileges. They could never be outside the view of a counselor and were not allowed to write home, unless to tell their parents they had done wrong and to outline how they would correct themselves. They were forced to write long lists about the things that led them to Swift River. A student could refuse to participate in any reprimand and face demotion back to Pathways or, worse, a return trip to wilderness or elsewhere.

When Avery and Brie finally arrived at the schoolhouse, they delayed a bit longer in the hallway until classes let out. Brie pointed out a few girls as her roommates and called them over. They were all white and pretty, and though the school was a mix of ethnicities and privilege, Avery felt remote and ostracized. The population was nearly equal parts girls to boys, rich and poor, East Coast and West Coast. Avery's feelings of self-worth had for some time been pinned to her relationships with her peers and how she was perceived. Now she felt like the black swan, without a proper place, somewhere in fact not many students belonged.

"This is Juliet, she's great, and she's in our room. She's from Florida," Brie said.

"What are you here for?" Juliet said.

"I didn't do anything," Avery said.

"Yeah, none of us did," Juliet said, tossing back her blonde hair. Avery noted how straight and perfect her hair seemed. Someone had a straightener.

"And this is Julia," Brie said. "Julia and Juliet, how fun! JJ. We should call you two JJ!"

"Where are you from?" Julia said.

"Boston," Avery said, then reconsidered. "Louisiana, actually. It's a long story."

"Everyone's story is long and boring," Julia said. "Good luck."

The two girls disappeared into a classroom down the hall, leaving Brie and Avery standing by the front doors.

"Julia hasn't been here very long," Brie said. "Just got here a few days ago."

"Everyone's here for eighteen months?"

"Don't get hung up on that," Brie said. "Things change."

Brie escorted Avery to the office where the program directors, Frank and Tanya, were meeting with Avery's godmother, whose face was now twisted in a permanent cry.

"We hope you liked the campus and what we have to offer here at Swift River," Tanya said. "Thank you for showing her around, Brie."

Before Brie left, she flashed a smile at Avery and handed her another soda bottle. It would be her last. Being caught with something as simple as a bottle of soda at Swift River was met with serious consequences. Brie's infraction, the unsolicited offering of a second soda to a newcomer, went unnoticed. Maybe it was forgiven. This simple act forged their friendship for the rest of their stay.

"We've just been here explaining the program to your godmother and what we aim to do with you while you're here, the goals we hope you'll accomplish, and what we'd like to see from you academically," Tanya said, closing the door behind Brie. "We're very excited you're here and hope you'll find your stay both rehabilitative and elucidating."

Avery didn't know the second word but knew the first well. Everyone had tried to rehabilitate her. She knew they wanted her to be better than she was, which seemed to her the same thing she wanted: to have not been raised in a household that stole her childhood. They wanted her to overcome a trauma toward which they had actively turned a blind eye. So she was not convinced this place, another place, would help.

Tanya went over admissions details, outlining the first bit of her program, which was the Pathways probationary period as Avery adjusted to the school. It meant no academic classes and very little interaction with anyone who wasn't in her orientation group or her therapy team.

Avery's godmother kept quiet, sobbing, her shoulders pumping in subtle rolling waves in the chair next to her. Avery would later recall her godmother as crying through "silent tears."

"I'm really, really sorry," her godmother finally said.

"I don't care," Avery shot back. "I'm never going to forgive you for this."

———

After Avery's godmother left, Brie returned to the office to get Avery, and they strolled together back along the corridor dominated by the large glass windows covered in mesh wiring. They were heading to the infirmary for her intake, which would be followed by her first therapy session. Avery recalled similar intakes, like the one in wilderness where they made her get naked and crouch in front of strangers who searched her for drugs and paraphernalia or contraband. Standing outside the infirmary, Avery heard a small yelp in the exam room. The door swung open and a nurse motioned her to enter as she made room for the departing boy, who grabbed his crotch in tears, having been subjected to a Q-tip swab straight into his urethra.

Two nurses told her to strip down to her underwear. She would take a pregnancy test in front of them. The staff had everything down to a science and made the interaction impersonal. "I'm also going to need you to take two fingers and run them through the bands of your bra and underwear," said Bailey, the nurse with a ruffled crop of auburn hair held in a bun.

"You're not allowed to have thongs, crop tops, spaghetti straps, tank tops," the other nurse said. "Do you have anything like that in your bags, because we're going to take that." And they did.

After her intake, Avery emerged from the room feeling just as violated as she had in her previous encounters with men. She decided this was okay because she was a bad person and bad people get treated badly for what they have done. *If I am bad,* she thought, *maybe this torment will turn me good.* This was more or less what the doctor told her when she sat for her initial psychiatry appointment. After a brief discussion of her personal history, including drug or alcohol use, promiscuity, and past relationships, and after forty-five minutes of hearing about her rape and penchant for self-harm, he diagnosed her with bipolar disorder and depression. He prescribed Prozac for her. She would receive a cocktail of prescriptions over the course of her two years at Swift River, beginning with the Prozac, an antidepressant, then expanding to Trileptal, for the treatment of bipolar disorder and epilepsy, and Abilify, also used in the treatment of bipolar disorder and schizophrenia. Soon her insomnia disappeared. With it went her desire to stand against the crushing weight of the program and the students in her therapy groups. She accepted everything without argument, a drone.

She continued with her therapy into the next few weeks in something of a trance. The school was divided into teams, which fell to different therapists, and so the next afternoon, Avery met the Cougar team therapist, Carmen. It was a group therapy session that took place after classes had finished for the day. "You know," Carmen said to the group gathered around her in chairs forming a circle in the Great Room, "hurt people hurt people."

Their experiences and traumas were different, yet they were all addressed as one. Avery missed the purpose of the group, which was to relate with a wider circle of people as a way for everyone to see they were not alone. Despite her medication, Avery felt alienated and alone, forced into a situation that made her uncomfortable. Nobody knew her; worst of all, Carmen did not know her, and yet, she still spoke with the assured poise of someone with answers. It made Avery more self-conscious, as though her problems were nothing but simple issues that could be talked away.

The group was loud.

"We already went over this and it wasn't my fault, it was my mom who started everything," screamed one young boy with a bowl haircut.

"This sounds familiar, Joey," Carmen said. "What do we think this sounds like?"

"You want me to fuckin' say it's fuckin' blame shifting, but that's some psychobabble bullshit that doesn't always work," Joey said. "You can't tell me what I know to be true. It wasn't me, can't you fuckin' see that?"

"No one's blaming you, Joey. We're on your side," Carmen said.

"Are you?" Joey said, rising from his seat. "You're a fuckin' bitch. I'm outa here."

He walked out through the door, slamming it behind him. Tense silence filled the room. He had broken an unspoken tenet of the program: smile and comply. He had not, and because of this Joey would not remain long at Swift River, whisked off to another program before any of his peers could speak with him in private.

Avery remembered a few other students who cast long shadows on her experience at the program. Some felt like they did not belong, some seemed like they were destined for much stricter, more-regimented programs, perhaps even jail. Avery befriended girls like her, dark girls, girls who were tormented in the past, girls who felt they were abandoned, all of whom loved to sing and dance. Between classes, when there were periods of open-gym time, while other students would climb the rock walls and shoot hoops on the basketball courts, Avery and her friends Molly and Rachel would practice dance routines. Despite her aversion to public performances, she and another friend were hoping to one night perform in the Great Room. The feelings she once had were still present, though tempered a bit by her medication. Given that she did enjoy the soft limelight given to her by male companions back home, she toyed with the dream of a room full of that same direct and allocated love.

Some days, as the weather continued inviting everyone outside, the ball games were brought onto blacktop courts, and Avery would drag a blanket out to the dandelion fields overlooking the basketball games. Avery, Molly, and Rachel would sit and sing, while a friend, Kat, strummed her guitar.

They would have lunch together and whisper about their treatment, gossiping about their therapists and recalling times when they enjoyed drugs or alcohol back home, how they hoped to return to that when they were released, to the boys and the parties and the makeup and dresses. On the outside, in the real world, they likely would not have talked or been friends. They all came from different backgrounds, and it was only Swift River that made them feel close, a forced connection most students felt while they were in the program. That false connection was reinforced by the student-to-student rules of interaction, which barred anyone from talking privately, from touching each other, from discussing their lives back home in detail. Tapping someone on the back or hugging them might lead the instructors to issue a ban between two people. Sometimes it was better to keep relationships just above the surface, in plain view, the way Avery and her group watched the boys shoot hoops from their blanket, the way they could dance together but alone.

But most times the sense of camaraderie forced Avery into trusting those she should not have. Relationships were prefaced on upholding appearances, even if they masked something sinister.

Doug was one of the kids whom Avery could never trust and also one who made her worried for her safety, unsure whether this program was as "soft" as it seemed; she felt that he was one of the boys who should be somewhere worse and more restrictive than Swift River. There were very mentally ill children who were not getting the care or supervision they needed, and Avery felt Doug fit that bill. He walked around school in a dark-blue floor-length robe. He acted like a prophet, whispering to himself in the halls, stopping to commune with the crown molding. He spoke in self-righteous diatribes, when not staring at a wall. The way he spoke down to Avery was not racist, but it was not far from it. He had been keen on Julia, the girl from Avery's dorm, but she broke up with him as his behavior became more antisocial. In the wreckage of their relationship (which blossomed, peaked, crashed, and burned in about a week), Doug had sat down to write a list of people he wished dead. He carried it around with him in his robe pocket and continued his muttering. Nothing ever came of the list. Still, people waited. Then, one night, an instructor patrolling the corridors came upon Doug in a bathroom, sitting on the toilet and ejaculating onto himself. He was covered in his own blood, which he had used as lubricant. He was kicked out of the program, whisked away overnight by three hulking men at two o'clock in the morning, never heard from again.

Most of the boys, though, were not like Doug. Many of them were really cute, as Brie had said. The girls always talked about boys they liked but were sure to never act upon it—or, at least, to never disclose it—for fear of being caught. Avery had her own fling very early in the program, which filled her emotional void with the attention of a boy. They briefly dated, a loose term associated with liking someone else on campus. They even kissed. They scooted off to an empty room in the school building and made out in the dark, making Avery feel loved and desired and all the things she missed about being home, the attention she could derive from just about anyone whose gaze was affixed onto her. She had long kept the secret and casually mentioned it one day to Molly, Rachel, and Kat. Avery felt safe telling them, but she was still new and did not yet know that word always got back to the therapists. Her first fling was quickly extinguished by a ban.

But then there was Greg. He came into her life like a comet, touching down into the burrows surrounding her heart and nestling there but never cooling. He had entered with the warmth of promise, that familiarity felt through belonging. Longevity seemed possible. For Avery, whose situation seemed more precarious after each meeting with Carmen, Greg saved her. A year older than she, he seemed to hold himself in no greater regard than the program did, which was to his benefit and helped him navigate the levels, based on his compliancy. He knew he was a wasted child and had no place in the world. He felt equally lost and at home amid the treatment plans and medications. He and Avery would sneak to the Great Room nightly to meet, and each time she felt like he was sent there, much in the way she felt toward Brie, to help prevent her from madness, a supplement to the medications she ingested each morning and night. She needed him, and the feeling was mutual. His beauty, to her, was simple. He did not work out, did not flex his muscles, but he was not overweight. Rather, he was the average boy of whom she had always dreamed. He was the boy next door, the one she never had. Best of all, he was from Massachusetts. She'd never felt so close to home.

He had captivating eyes and a "really pretty smile." He understood Avery in a way few others could. In his own family, he was the black sheep. He, like Avery, could not understand his rampant and erratic emotions, which he often could not articulate and felt were the reason his parents despised him. "That's where our friendship blossomed," Avery said.

At Swift River, the two swapped notes. "Me and Greg became a thing," Avery said years later. Their notes were innocent at first, veering into the romantic and serious, climaxing at the explicit and erotic. "We were sexting before sexting was a thing," Avery said. "We talked a lot of shit about people." The words and thoughts grew into things, and they engaged each other physically, sometimes in the school building's photography darkroom or with their hands beneath a table at dinner. "When our friends found out about it, they were, like, 'Are you fucking kidding me? We were sitting there eating.' They were not happy." But Greg and Avery were.

One day, as they waited among their group of friends in the Great Room, a Swift River admissions brochure and packet that someone had pilfered from a therapist's office was passed around. Fading in and out of the conversation before her, Avery recalled the brochures her godmother gave her while in wilderness, which outlined the other programs and the stricter treatment she could receive.

"This is what they want us to look like," Greg told her, as they looked at the photos in the pamphlets advertising Swift River. "This kid, the one holding up that fish, he got kicked out before you got here. And look, there's Carlos," he said, pointing out another student in the photos. "He's been here forever. He said that they told him to smile or they'd lengthen his program."

"They said that to him?"

"They tried to scare him into it. Now, when I'm told to smile, I'll ask for cash," Greg went on. "If not that, then I'll settle for one of those sodas they give you at orientation."

"So good," Avery said.

She knew that any hint of a relationship would separate them. It would prolong their stay. It would trigger a series of events that would fling them into a never-ending therapeutic damnation. So she kept her distance, watching the prospect of a different sort of family materialize, one which she came to cherish—and then lose.

2

Please take advantages [*sic*] of the resources there at [Swift River] . . . I met Carmen, your therapist, today briefly. She seems pretty nice . . . Don't forget you still need to write a responsibility letter. I did not read one from you.

—Avery's godmother, excerpt from letter to Avery

From the outside, Swift River may have looked idyllic; on the inside, Avery—like so many others—found it oppressive. The school structure became the model of myriad other behavior-modification programs—stricter lockdown facilities and tangential wilderness programs. (Swift River, which was owned by Aspen Education Group, had its own wilderness therapy component until the school began encouraging parents to first send their children to a dedicated wilderness program.) Around the American heartland, these programs were cropping up like cornstalks. Many used corporal punishment, isolation practices, and threats against students that extended into their worlds back home.

What was taught and learned at one institution was often borrowed by others, if not in the same corporate ecosystem, then in the same health care system. Though the names of punishments might change ("challenges" in one program might be called "opportunities" in another program), the ethos remained. Whereas one program in Massachusetts might enroll clients with fewer behavioral issues, another would welcome "difficult" clients who they might then restrain or pacify with sedatives. Schools like Swift River were billed as boarding schools—less restrictive than lockdowns or residential treatment facilities, which were akin to rehabilitation centers or low-security prisons—if only to ease a parent's worry about the safety of their child.

Many of the clients with whom I spoke found it difficult to articulate how exactly a residential program had harmed them. Much of what they experienced seemed innocuous in the retelling. Set against the ostensible beauty of the school, the clients likewise could not reconcile their emotions with their surroundings. How could they be sad in a place of relative tranquility? What harm could come from being forced to treat their parents with respect in letters home? They were at least thankful they could communicate with one another, which was more than they could do in wilderness therapy. What was so wrong about being told to not have romantic relationships when they were sent away to focus on themselves, not someone else? They were still able to spend time with the opposite gender. And how could writing your life story be a detriment? At least they had this one creative outlet.

There are serious long-term consequences for being censored and told to repress emotional or sexual desires. Like living in a police state, such controlling atmospheres tend to slowly taint the view of one's self-worth. Patients begin to question how terrible they were in the first place and begin to vilify, rather than victimize, themselves. They become self-loathing and self-deprecating. They begin to believe they are more bad than good and therefore should not be alive at all. The patients begin to internalize all the censorship. In the years that follow, if someone tells them they are loved or that they are doing good work, they often cannot accept it. A child is then defined not by lessons learned but by mistakes made. Punishments for mishaps become a vicious cycle and a product born of the self-loathing. Their lives will never extend beyond the catastrophe of their adolescence.

The therapeutic approach championed by Swift River and other facilities like it included a wealth of behavior-modification techniques, of which cognitive behavioral therapy (CBT) was a part. CBT examines how someone's thoughts become things or actions. CBT-oriented therapists may use Rhonda Byrne's book *The Secret* (often used in both wilderness and residential programs), which chronicles how what a person puts into the universe—physically, metaphysically, emotionally, through karma—is what they will receive in return. *Be kind to others and receive only kindness. Do no harm and have no harm done unto you.* This type of therapy was created in the 1960s to help treat depression. The therapy was found effective in preventing relapse among alcoholics and was further adapted for people addicted to harder drugs and those who had behavioral issues.

Dialectic behavior therapy (DBT), which focuses on resolving the seeming contradiction between self-acceptance and change, is also prevalent at these institutions. The method is something like a war of attrition against whatever reasons someone has for drinking or abusing drugs. Why, if you are so mad at the world, would you take it out on yourself? If drinking is meant to ease your suffering, why is it causing you more suffering?

The people who designed these modalities did not realize that self-harm was often the point.

———

The effectiveness of the therapy offered at residential treatment facilities is not the reason such places exist. The "residential" aspect is often the most appealing factor, because it signals an intensive focus on the child's needs and a removal of external influencers that, in the past, have caused the client to stray. In both affluent and poorer areas of the United States, parents agree that teenagers have less support than they did a generation before. Many public schools resemble factories that turn out students who think not for their edification but, rather, only for their grade, and few communities have adults around in the afternoon—leaving children in the hands of babysitters or alone. Teenagers from all income and ethnic backgrounds fall through the cracks for a variety of reasons, but modern parents face issues that past generations did not: designer drugs seem more dangerous and prevalent in the lives of children; computers, phones, and video games have taken the place of playdates; through the internet, it is possible to learn about and connect with nearly everything untoward.

Hundreds of special schools began opening across the country in the 1970s, the schools becoming more prevalent as struggles born of the later technological era developed in tandem. Called emotional growth or therapeutic schools, they are Spartan versions of traditional boarding schools. They remove students from a toxic environment—a home where they clash with their parents, a high school where they experience bullying, a neighborhood where they hang out with drug dealers—and offer adult role models and a new set of peers. Students' schedules are crammed with academic classes, exercise, and six or more hours a week of group therapy. Counselors lead seminars on time management, responsible sexual behavior, and addictions.

The special schools form the second sector of a multifaceted, once-burgeoning but still-present private industry that began in the mid-twentieth century with Synanon, a rehabilitation program after which many of today's residential treatment centers for teenagers are modeled and one that was founded on the principle that conventional therapy was not enough. They differed from their wilderness counterparts by reintroducing the clients to normal social atmospheres and allowing access to the outside world and FI, while still enrolled in intensive therapy.

People who joined Synanon to overcome addiction were drawn to unconventional pseudoscience modalities for therapy. Synanon was founded in Santa Monica, California, in 1958 by Charles Dederich, a University of Notre Dame dropout and member of Alcoholics Anonymous. After participating in an LSD experiment conducted by UCLA professor Dr. Keith Ditman, Dederich decided to create a group that embraced all types of afflictions, rather than isolating addictions, giving rise to Synanon's two-year residential program shortly after.

In the 1960s, reception of the group was positive. Many celebrities—Jane Fonda and Leonard Nimoy, among others—were spotted at Synanon headquarters, where actors, writers, musicians, and politicians mingled in recovery and sobriety. Dederich subsequently expanded the organization from a storefront to an armory and later to a beachside hotel. This became the headquarters and main residence for inpatients during treatment, though Dederich would shed the two-year model for something more permanent: a lifelong membership. Dederich thought that full recovery was impossible and, in turn, so was graduation.

By 1968, the group had approximately eleven hundred members and was receiving millions of dollars in donations. The group expanded throughout California and into Nevada, New York, and Puerto Rico. Dormitories were added so that members could live together. So successful was the program, California judges began referring juvenile offenders to Synanon.

The program's renown hinged on the Synanon Game, a form of group attack therapy in which members would open up about themselves only to be met with a barrage of criticism and verbal abuse. Patients targeted one another with vicious harassment and ridicule, often aiming to elicit a response from their peers. Attack therapy sessions occurred in individual or group therapy with the goal of tearing down an individual's ego to create a foundation from which they could build themselves up. In this highly confrontational setting, some individuals fared better than others.

The game was essential to Dederich's strategy for rehabilitation; members were meant to be "scared straight" into sobriety. The emotional damage done by the game far outweighed its benefits, however. Synanon was eventually discredited for the psychological trauma it inflicted on participants. Synanon members publicly confronted the violent nature of the organization, accusing it of child abuse, assault, and, in one case, wrongful imprisonment by a former patient who felt held against her will.

By the early 1980s, Synanon—and its "terror and violence"—was better known for its controversies than its successes. After Synanon failed to reorganize as a religion, the Internal Revenue Service questioned its appropriation of donations and stripped the cult-like group of its tax-exempt status. The company folded in 1991, and Dederich died from heart failure in 1997.

But, by the 1990s, Synanon had spurred offshoots that mirrored attack therapy. Among the more notable programs were Healthcare America (formerly the Brown Schools, Inc.); CEDU Educational Services, which was founded by a former member of Synanon named Mel Wasserman in 1967; and the Élan School, which opened in 1970 in Poland, Maine, and was initially and often the subject of allegations of abuse. The Élan School, unlike the other descendants of Synanon, worked more specifically with teenagers with behavioral problems. If CEDU was a watered-down version of Synanon, Élan was the concentrate. One notable alumnus, Michael Skakel, made headlines as the Kennedys' cousin who killed Martha Moxley on October 30, 1975. With the case making national headlines twenty-five years after the actual murder took place, memories of the Élan School resurfaced, and many accounts of the horrors that took place became known. One account, in the *Hartford Courant*, described how Skakel was "beaten to his knees in a boxing ring by a succession of students." Another student was paddled to the point of hospitalization. When faced with these accusations, Élan School officials did not deny them (except for the allegations of spanking)—they were explained away as safer-than-they-sound practices.

In 1997, Healthcare America operated fourteen facilities, "including centers that offer independent private school, residential services, in-home outpatient and therapeutic foster care." The organization saw an opportunity to use a $31 million buyout to reinvest in the at-risk youth business under its former name, the Brown Schools. One research analyst for Equitable Securities Corporation said at the time, "There's going to be more kids who are troubled or at risk, and there's greater demand than ever for the type of services that Brown Schools offers."

As part of its expansion into the troubled-teen industry, Brown Schools acquired CEDU in 1998 for $78 million. The union of these two organizations was meant to demonstrate that the Brown Schools had "significantly strengthened its commitment to children and their families."

They were a perfect match. CEDU was "at its peak in the market" at the time it was bought. But, within the first two years of its acquisition, "the staff turnover at the highest level was unbelievable." While operational, the Brown Schools were responsible for a combination of private and public schools, from which they profited off tuition and government contracts with school districts and juvenile detention centers. In the decades that the Brown Schools invested in publicly funded juvenile treatment, a primary focus since its founding in 1940, its affiliates were connected to multiple deaths due to restraint or seclusion. A 2005 *Dateline* episode examined the deaths of five Brown Schools students, specifically the 2002 death of Chase Moody, the son of a former Brown Schools defense attorney. Several former employees, including once–chief executive officer John Harcourt Jr., went on to work at Camelot Schools, another for-profit school, as the splintering continued.

CEDU, like the Brown Schools, rose from the ashes of its former organization to restore itself among the vanguard in the at-risk youth industry. With over three decades of operation before its acquisition, its legacy all but developed the private-pay residential programs industry. Although CEDU operated under Brown Schools for a number of years, it is widely credited with founding the private therapeutic schools industry. It is also more vividly remembered for the nightmarish therapy techniques that left hundreds of its students traumatized and would be the subject of continuing lawsuits.

———

Over the ensuing years, many residential troubled-teen programs have been exposed as violent, but families continue to send their children—and their money—to such institutions. At its peak operation in 2010, Universal Health Services, Inc., operated more than two hundred behavioral health facilities in thirty-seven states, Puerto Rico, and the Virgin Islands, including residential programs for youth and juvenile detention centers. Its Behavioral Health division alone produced revenues of $3.4 billion.

Clients who find themselves first attending wilderness before a residential program are often placed on a trajectory encouraged by educational consultants, a small group of advisers who frequently operate in a niche market of affluence and desperation. Likewise, the residential programs encourage parents to send their children to a wilderness program before enrollment. The three groups complement each other, sometimes collaborating on treatment plans that keep clients in the system.

Residential programs across the country are at times the subject of large civil inquiries. Some complaints against the staff at CEDU's various facilities ranged from allegations that "one boy was forced to dig a grave and lie in a closed coffin while staff members tossed dirt on it" to calling students "degrading names such as 'whore' and 'fatty.'" Lawsuits often claimed that the staff at CEDU facilities lacked training and were abusive. Riots, like one at the Academy at Ivy Ridge in 2005, sometimes broke out. In 1997, a two-hour riot at Northwest

Academy in Idaho left five students injured. There were also at least three known child disappearances from CEDU programs between 1993 and 2004. James Lee Crummel, the convicted California serial killer, frequented a CEDU campus, where he often accompanied the program's psychiatrist, Burnell Forgey. Such controversies and a lack of proper funding were the impetus for many program closures, including Brown Schools' CEDU facilities in 2005. Only three of CEDU's facilities were reopened by Universal Health Services: the Ascent Program, Boulder Creek Academy, and Northwest Academy. In 2018, Northwest Academy shut its doors, citing low enrollment.

Accounts of abuse and neglect emerge frequently in civil courts and on the internet, which is why Élan School owner Sharon Terry blamed online attacks for the school's eventual shuttering on April 1, 2011. As with other offshoots of Synanon, the basis for closure was the use of harsh behavior-modification techniques, despite the owner of Élan School, like Northwest Academy, citing "declining enrollment and resulting financial difficulties." *Mother Jones* reported "only ten to fifteen percent of the [clients] who participated in these techniques recovered," but it is likely that many of them felt broader psychological harms, which in the end is tough for investigators to prove and even harder for prosecutors to try in court.

Whether the program was wilderness, residential, lockdown, or something more nefarious, labels hardly mattered to the teenagers sent there, since all the therapy programs focused on similar treatment. What did matter was that the false sense of freedom gained from progressing out of wilderness and into a residential program was used as leverage to get students to comply with program rules. If they succeeded, they were told, they might return home sooner.

Throughout their time in whatever program, little could be done to reverse the effects of that first night when they were stripped of their former lives. One day they were at home with friends, the next they were tossed together, their connections to family and home severed overnight. "It was either give in or suffer. They pick you apart as a person, and when you give in, they help build you back up," said Kevin, a student who attended Swift River after a lockdown residential treatment center known as Island View, the subject of an investigation by the *Huffington Post*, which publicized the child-neglect practices of an Aspen Education Group institution. "It was an aggressive approach."

The issue at each troubled program was never its troubled clientele. The programs were often staffed with inexperienced counselors with untraceable or disqualifying credentials for handling young people. Further complicating matters was the single treatment modality deployed for a range of very complex neurological and behavioral issues: psychological treatment billed as an all-in-one Hail Mary. One child with schizophrenic tendencies might be treated in the same way as someone who suffered from acute social phobias like anxiety or depression. Plans were billed as individually tailored, but many of them suggested the same treatment route: intensive group and individual therapy with the occasional prescribed antidepressant. Instead of an individual diagnosis, every child was urged to stay at the program for as long as possible and try a host of prescription medication intermixed with hikes and home visits. The tuition and other bills mounted. Families who were not so financially privileged borrowed money or refinanced their homes.

Meanwhile, the students faced fixing their own problems alone. They rarely distinguished what their problems were. Were they actually angry and entitled? Or had they a right to be mad for being kidnapped? Was their frustration justified if their parents had abandoned them? Were they wrong to feel alone and sad in a new world not of their choosing? Did they deserve to be treated so harshly by the program staff?

Abuse is not always physical. Part of the tough-love tool kit promoted by schools like Swift River were simple rules and words, directions and demands, enforced by intimidation or immediate physical, emotional distress, to say nothing of the psychological effects of being shunted from wilderness programs to residential programs, seeing your family very rarely, and not knowing what exactly it will take to get you home. Even in the years that followed the program, many students would have trouble articulating their experience as abuse.

But it *was* abuse. Rules and systems that seemed benign then—like facing isolation for spreading a rumor, eating alone in the communal dining spaces, being told that the only way to get home was by moving up the system of levels constructed like military ranks—were humiliating and tormented the students. "Rap groups," as some programs called them, were what Swift River had for group therapy: open and confrontational groups during which peers would hold others accountable, often in angry verbal outbursts. Students feared touching anyone because the programs ingrained in them that doing so might trigger a person's past trauma. Students could not trust their friends or family because the school prized accountability, and so the students began to fear that entrusting someone with a secret or wrongdoing might spell their own demise. Thus, rarely did the students form meaningful relationships with each other.

The psychologist Robert Jay Lifton's thought-reform studies into brainwashing and mind control touch on some of the techniques used in programs like Swift River: milieu control severs communication with the outside world (save for letters to and from parents or guardians) and redirects thinking to the ideology presented immediately before the individual; confession of past sins requires the individual to place trust in the group and its higher purpose, which is made to seem altruistic and above the outside world through mystical manipulation; self-sanctification through purity encourages the individual to push toward an unattainable perfection—as in cults, the pursuit of perfection will promote the individual to higher levels within the group, which are meaningless. The children are made to believe that the levels are the most important achievements they can make, that they represent their emotional and mental well-being. The children are told to bare all to the other students and the instructors. They are made to write and rewrite and write again their past mistakes, to relive them over and over, until they see the errors of their ways. They are taught to give up their control over their lives—their appearance, their physical possessions—in order to be made whole.

3

There are so many things we need to talk about! I am ready
to work on myself, my family, my life. So I am looking forward to the therapy sessions with Carmen & at home too.
I am looking forward to learning what you learn regarding
adoption & dealing with it—that was never something I
focused on in my own therapy, so I am interested in learning from you. Know that I love you, and always will, no
matter how angry I have been. Please take advantage of
the resources there at ASR [Academy at Swift River], the
therapy, the activities—they are precious gifts that most
people who need them never have access to . . .

—Avery's godmother, excerpt from letter to Avery

E ighteen months, give or take," Carmen had told Avery when
she asked how long she would stay at Swift River. "Not everybody's the same."

Over time, though, it became clear that Carmen wanted Avery to
stay until she turned eighteen years old. She would extend Avery's program length twice, saying that Avery was not ready to return to society.

The extensions of her stay aside, nothing about Swift River fundamentally worried Avery. She remembered the television shows in which rowdy juveniles were locked up in prison to get a taste of the consequences of their actions. *At least it's not that,* she thought.

One night, back during Avery's first week, the school gathered in the Great Room. "Stand up and tell the room who you are," the counselor instructed the students in the room. Avery later described the experience as taking part in a public confessional. She stood before the student body in the dark, moonlit Great Room and began to speak. She didn't want to recount her life story, share with strangers her problems and issues, even if that was what they expected. The order of the evening was to maintain as much control as she could over what life she still held. She shared what she could, then sat down.

As days then weeks slipped by and she became more involved in the therapy, Avery took an inventory of her issues. She wanted to give the program a fair chance at helping her. She noted to herself that she both distrusted men and needed them. Even when they were abusive, she would use men to help boost her self-esteem.

She noted that her problems included an unwillingness to communicate that she felt lost, but even when she practiced saying this in her head, it sounded weird, disingenuous. She'd already known everyone was faking his or her own way through the program, so that was what she would try to do, at least in the beginning.

Later that first month, one afternoon much like many others in those first few days, she finished her therapy and schoolwork—composed of writing lists of dos and don'ts and memorizing the names of staff members and in which rooms particular groups met—and made her way back to her room before dinner. Avery washed her face in the multisink bathroom she shared with the other girls in her dorm. She wet her face and opened her small shower bag on the white countertop between two of the four sinks. It contained semblances of her life back home, small pleasures she still maintained: shampoo, conditioner, soap, toothpaste. She took things slow, appreciating the things she was prohibited from having in the wilderness. First she dabbed some cleanser into her hand, then scrubbed the cream into neat spirals that soon began to foam. She applied the cleanser as though it were a ritual, a catharsis against the shrieking of girls in the rooms around her, getting ready for dinner the best she could without makeup.

After dinner, Avery returned to the cottage to again look at herself in the mirror, always finding bits of time in which she could try to center herself. She desired to change, unlike some of the girls and boys there. Her groups were full of people trying to meet the program's standards through disingenuous subterfuge. She knew this, the therapists knew this, and still everyone acted like the therapy was working fine. Avery kept trying, despite her encounters with others. Liam, also in the Cougar therapy group, was one of the fakers. Circled up in a room with the doors and windows closed, like prison but with an added air of emotional vulnerability, Avery sat across from Liam during one of their twice-weekly sessions with Carmen.

"I just wanted to start this group with an open floor, allowing anyone to speak freely or discuss matters that have been on their mind," Carmen began. "It's important to let everything out, not keep it inside, which oftentimes can serve as a distancing method, pushing us further from the people who want to help us."

Everyone sat still, trading glances but peering out the window as a bird alighted on the windowsill.

"It's not being vulnerable or weak, which is something I've discussed with a few of you in our private sessions," Carmen said. "It's about trust and honesty, which, as the cliché goes, has that wonderful ability to let us free."

"Set," a boy said from the corner of the room.

"That's good," Carmen said. "Speak up. What was it you wanted to say, Porter?"

"I said, 'set.'"

"Set what?"

"Honesty can *set* us free, not *let* us free."

"Yes," Carmen said, ignoring the young man's rebuke. "Yes, it can."

Avery took note. She liked how Carmen handled the boy's rejoinder with aplomb: she would try a similar tactic in the future, Avery promised herself. Carmen looked around the room, surveying the confused faces, many of whom she believed might one day graduate, go on to college, a career. Avery saw little promise in anyone, which made her even more determined to succeed. She liked Brie: yes, she had been kind and jovial and supportive on that first day, but as she got to know the routines of other students, she began to see much of the treatment and the students' "change" as nothing more than a lie.

"I have something I want to say," Liam chimed in. "It's about Avery, who I feel is just pushing back against all the hard work everyone is doing."

Avery did not know why she was being called out. Her face drained of blood, and then she turned red with anger. She hardly spoke to Liam, in the group or outside of it. He was one of the upperclassmen at Level Four, close to going home and supposedly a model student, though Avery knew he had made a mortar and pestle out of clay in art class to crush the pills he stole from the infirmary.

"You probably are worried about the therapy, and lemme say, we all were as Pathways students, Level Ones," Liam continued, borrowing from the language of the program, a common tactic for someone who was geared toward gaming the system and hoping to leave ahead of his scheduled program. He sounded more like a therapist than himself, the boy who everyone knew to be drinking hand sanitizer at night. The gel solution was often diluted in water bottles and carried around without suspicion from the counselors or therapists. A few quick pumps of a hand sanitizer dispenser into a water bottle went unnoticed. Soon some students stole the bags right out of the pumps and returned them nearly emptied. This may seem like the desperation of addicts, but it was more because the students felt insecure and knew only this way to bond. After all, if they often lionized their actions back home, they had to prove their mettle here at the programs too.

"You probably just have to start being really honest with yourself and get with the program," Liam said, staring Avery down.

He and others she knew would call her and other students out for wrongdoing, "literally in front of everyone," Avery said years later. She and Liam hardly knew each other, but he called out Avery as a way to show his therapists what they wanted to see: change and maturation, however false or fabricated. He did not need to know her to make her his prey. "I know you're snorting pills, like, come on," Avery said of the encounter years later. "But it happened a lot, and that was the whole thing with the program. After you learn about what it means to advance through the levels, you put other people under the bus—that's when you get to go home, and that's why I never made it out of that program." Carmen allowed Avery to respond, and she said she was thankful for the constructive feedback, responding with restraint like she had observed in Carmen.

Sitting and brooding in another corner of the group was Julia. She had struggled to make friends, even after finishing Pathways with Avery and Doug, and had also found it difficult to advance through the levels. She was not doing well in group or individualized therapy sessions, continually combative and frustrated with being gone from home.

"How have you been adjusting to the program, your roommates, Julia?" Carmen said.

She heaved a heavy sigh.

"I don't want to be here," she said.

"That's totally natural," Carmen said and leaned back. "I'm sure everyone here has felt that way at some point."

A hysteria of giggles and snorts rippled through the students, then silence.

"Yeah, maybe, but, like, I am going to do whatever I have to do to get out of here," Julia said through gritted teeth. Carmen took this as determination, not a portent.

"You'll work the program and be just fine," Carmen said, unaware of Julia's intentions. "Baby steps."

"Yeah," Julia said. "Something like that."

———

Avery had been at Swift River for roughly eight months. Every so often, administrators passed around a Truth List. If the instructors heard through the student rumor mill that someone had broken one of the agreements—sexual acts, stealing, drinking—students would be separated and asked to reveal all they knew on an informal loose-leaf sheet of paper sent to each student in the school. Administrators could not indict someone without proof, so they schemed to make the students turn on each other. On the lined paper, students filled out acts of sex or violence or any other rule breaking—even just poor thoughts, bad thinking, or bad intentions that the students themselves had had or had heard of someone else considering.

When Avery was passed a Truth List, she found herself confronting the truths she kept inside and had not yet grappled with openly, with Carmen or any of her friends. Avery was sitting in the lunchroom at a table all to herself. The student body had been separated and told they could not speak until the last Truth List was returned to the staff. She knew of so many things that could get others in trouble, and she knew a Truth List would not be going around simply because the staff were fishing. They knew something. And that something often meant expulsion from the program into worse programs—another incentive to behave and cooperate. Avery thought of her relationship with Greg, which had sprouted into something unimaginable, even, Avery would say, wonderful. She was unsure of whether they were targeting them and their relationship or if it might be something else, like Liam's pill usage.

It was this Truth List that ended Greg and Avery for good. "I am broken," Avery said to me later. "[Because of those lists,] I tell on myself whenever I do anything. I don't sit with guilt. I didn't know if they knew about us or not, but I did not want to deal with Carmen if they did." When Avery saw Greg with a Truth List, she convinced herself that the administrators suspected something between them, despite the whole school working through their own version of a list.

How the list came about was this: When the students were out of their dorms, whether in therapy or at school, the staff might rummage through their rooms in search of contraband. Sometimes a "chill" staff member would warn the girls ahead of a check, but this time no one had warned Avery or Greg. Administrators discovered a cache of love notes between the two in Greg's room, which led them to find more in Avery's.

Carmen called Avery into her office.

"Why do you continue to break the sex agreement?" Carmen said, recalling the time when Avery had been caught kissing a different boy, before she met Greg. "Why do you do this even though you know it's against the rules?"

Avery thought, *Because it's a stupid rule for a teenager.* But she knew what Carmen wanted to hear.

"It just became ingrained in me at such a young age that men basically define your worth, so without one, who are you?" She had learned from Liam to say what she believed everyone wanted to hear, borrowing words she would never otherwise speak, words she hoped would get her home.

Carmen smiled, knowing she was being fed a line.

"Tell me how you really feel."

Avery thought for a moment before she said, "Because I love him."

"Let's talk more about that. You and Greg are never going to talk again after you have both completed this program. The people you meet here and the relationships you build here are not real. You are in a puddle, and you have to choose from these people. There are no other choices. If you were back in society, the pool would be bigger and you would never choose from these kids, would you?"

Avery recalled that conversation nearly a decade later and said, "Thinking back on that, that's a really fucked-up way to teach kids how to love," as though it were a transaction. (When students at Swift River later learned that couples in the program had begun to date after they graduated, a group of Carmen's students went to her and asked if she remembered what she had told them about relationships after treatment, how they were never going to care about those people. "Well, we will see how long those last," Carmen said.)

The morning after her meeting with Carmen about the Truth List, Avery went down to breakfast. She sat at her regular table and waited for Greg. When he never arrived, her friends told her over wet, soggy eggs that, overnight, Greg had been escorted back to a wilderness program.

"I was a mess," Avery said. "I was absolutely heartbroken, and then the guilt of not being sent away, while I [had done] the same thing as him, that hurt too. When I asked Carmen about it, she said either I was going back or he was. I guess they felt like I would do better at Swift River. I don't know."

———

The next morning, Avery walked to class thinking of Greg. Her teacher, Mr. Dushanbe, taught a lesson on Oxford commas, during which Avery struggled to stay awake as he droned on. She briefly caught sight of someone she thought was Greg in the hallway. It was not him, of course, but her heart was instantaneously hooked twice: once by the fleeting thoughts of love, then again by abandonment and shame.

At lunch, she ate and watched another girl, who had arrived recently from a wilderness therapy program in upstate New York, sit at a table alone with a stack of papers. She had been caught kissing a boy, too, and had already been placed on a restriction: no talking or eating with other students until she finished the paperwork, which comprised piercing questions about her sexuality and intentions in life and love. *Now there's a girl I can get along with,* Avery thought. She had started finding comfort in knowing she could break the rules and find others doing the same. There was safety, or at the very least commiseration and its company, in numbers.

That evening, before the students gathered after dinner in the Great Room for their nightly meeting, some girls lounged at the cottage reading *A Million Little Pieces* or *Harry Potter and the Deathly Hallows*, while others gossiped about their fellow students. Avery wore a plain gray pullover sweater, as impersonal as her feelings toward the counselors and the program. Then, at the direction of a counselor, everyone made their way to the Great Room. Avery sat down next to her friends, Molly and Rachel, who had saved her a seat on one of the green couches with the scratchy fabric. As she waited for the meeting to begin, she noticed that Julia was still not in the Great Room. "Everybody notices if somebody is missing. If somebody is not at meeting, the whole school knows. When you go up to the Great Room and you are trying to act like everything is all normal, then . . . you were just missing and somebody else is still missing and your roommates are, like, what's going on, what's going on, where is Julia?"

"I've to run back and grab something," Avery said, without asking. The staff members with their radios threw their hands up in brief frustration and waited at the entrance to the Great Room as she ran off back to the dorms. When Avery darted into the cottage, she did not catch sight of Julia. Her heart quickened. The living room, which had seemed large many times before, now felt claustrophobic. Down through a flight of steps to Julia's bedroom and into the quiet, darkened space. Julia's bed was along a wall nearest the window, and there was a bunk bed adjacent to hers against the other wall. Avery checked the back of the room for Julia. Nothing. Then she saw a closet half open. She called for Julia, but she did not answer. She walked closer and reached out for the closet door. The floor creaked beneath the carpet, as though talking in whispers.

Avery hoped and feared Julia was in there. She pulled open the closet, but Julia was not there either.

Avery, relieved not to find Julia in the closet but still concerned, left the room and again entered the living room, passing the couches and recliners, heading for the shared bathroom along the far end of the lower floor. The bathroom door was shut, but a strip of light crowned the doorjamb. Avery knew the lights had been turned off behind the girls, so she carefully and tentatively pushed open the door. Beyond the sinks were two shower stalls against the wall. One stall's curtain seemed mangled, pushed to the side, covered in blood. She saw Julia slumped over inside.

Suddenly Avery could see that blood was everywhere in the room, cast across the mirrors and curtains and sinks, which seemed so far from the shower. Avery bounded across the room. She dropped to the floor and examined Julia's wrists. Julia sobbed, her chest falling but never quite rising, like that of a tired bird. The blood was bright red and thick and turning darker. It seemed to Avery impossible to stanch the flow. Soon they were crying together. Julia was barely awake as Avery cradled her on the shower stall floor.

"I am so sorry," Avery said, sitting now in the puddle of blood by Julia. "I'm sorry, I'm so sorry." She grabbed at Julia's wrists, trying to stop what had already begun.

Avery screamed for help. The girls rocked together on the floor.

Two counselors quickly appeared in the bathroom doorway, survey-ing the chaos.

"I knew something was going to h-h-happen when she spoke in g-g-group the other day," Avery told them, crestfallen and crying. "She said something was going to happen, but I-I-I never—" Avery knew the reason. Avery had cut herself often, but never so deep or with a terminal goal. She almost sympathized with Julia. It was not a large leap from constant scrutiny to self-loathing to suicidal ideation. Avery had felt the same during her own self-studies and restrictions, during which she had to write the story of her first love. She wrote that story so many times that it soon felt like it was not hers but a story about someone else. Whereas it first might have been about a girl in love with a boy, a girl who would do anything for that boy, her story ended up sounding more like a young prostitute poaching young men who wanted her only for her body. Her life seemed like someone else's performance, she a bit player. The narrative she had told herself for so long—that she was not the problem but, rather, the product of bad situations—was changing at the hands of the program. Her life story no longer made sense and disturbed her. Had she been crazy all along? Had she never seen the truth? Were all these strangers, the ones telling her she was nearly a prostitute, right? She couldn't differentiate between what was real and what was a fabrication of the program. It was enough to wish yourself dead.

One of the counselors, Nate, grabbed Avery off the floor. He dragged her past the blood-covered sinks and mirrors. Through the bathroom door they stumbled into the cottage living room. Avery collapsed on the floor again, sobbing and screaming.

"She didn't w-w-want to be here," Avery continued, as she struggled against Nate, a man, a man touching her forcibly. "She said she was g-g-going to do whatever she had to do to get out, and you, you don't just, you don't do that," she said and motioned her hand across her wrist.

One of the nurses entered the cottage and bolted past Avery and Nate through the bathroom door, closing it behind her. Nate tried to see whether Avery was bleeding too. Julia's blood covered her khakis and gray sweatshirt. Several minutes passed, and when Avery had calmed

KENNETH R. ROSEN

down, Nate asked her to change her clothes. Once she had changed, he sent her back to the Great Room. "Don't say anything," he told her.

She walked back into the Great Room, where the evening meeting was concluding and a counselor was going over the room-cleaning schedule for each team. A girl was dying on the bathroom floor less than one hundred feet away and the meeting still carried on, Avery thought. She sat with Molly and Rachel, crying hysterically into her sweater, trying to hide her outburst, trying to rack her brain for how this could have happened. No one could have razors or sharp materials for this reason. They all but confiscated shoelaces one week to prevent a suspected hanging attempt. "What's going on?" Molly said. "Where's Julia?" Rachel asked.

The next morning, Julia's stuff would be gone, her bunk empty.

"What we didn't see very often were situations like Julia's. Where somebody actually tries to kill themselves and not just running away or drinking hand sanitizer or snorting their meds or something," Avery reflected. Everyone assumed that Julia had been taken to the hospital and later admitted to a psych ward. But since the students were practiced at maintaining their lives in the present, no one was ever sure what became of their roommate, the girl who had made a promise and followed through.

For the rest of her stay at Swift River, as Avery sat in groups or in her science or English classes or at one of the three daily meals, she looked down at her own arms, which were crosshatched with shallow cuts, each line once a breath of fresh air, a release. She had not considered cutting for a while; but now the sensation returned, and she toyed with the idea of again picking up the habit. When she needed emotional replenishment, she would reach for anything sharp. Never a razor blade—just anything that could break the skin and summon beads of blood. She recalled the broken CD she used back home to release whatever invisible toxins welled in her sink. The moment was always something special, comparing every cut to a hit of something stronger.

In Avery's mind, she began to fantasize about this release. She was almost jealous of Julia. She remembered how good she once felt, unlike now. "My cuts were shallow. They were specifically just to make me feel better . . . and get through that moment," she said, "like Julia's."

———

Several months later, Avery watched from her seat as Tom, a cherubic little blond-haired boy, chewed his gum and flashed a smile beneath his graduation cap and gown. The graduation music was the normal mix of uplifting and inspirational instrumentals, but the graduation was anything but normal. It felt awkward and staged, almost deceptive. The presentation of students and staff felt forced. The eyes of the children seemed dulled, their faces devoid of expression, their hearts full of agony, arms empty.

Tom, Liam, and the other graduates nevertheless bumped fists with one another and smiled and jostled in their seats. Behind them sat the rest of the student body in suits and summer dresses.

It was hot. The collars of the young boys soaked through and began staining gray with sweat. The students in the back, where Avery was sitting, were not going home. And they made a game of guessing whose parents belonged to which graduate, judging by nose protrusions or hair color, making cruel jokes about how the girls will end up gross like their mothers.

Frank, the school director, took the stage. His eyes were droopy. He was emotionally exhausted and beaten by the heat. There was much more on his mind. The ceremony would be for him less a commencement than an unburdening. He seemed nervous, hands trembling, eyes darting.

"It always amazes me what parents have to do to send their children off to schools like ours. It takes an incredible amount of courage and faith, and I thank you for putting your trust in us," Frank began.

"Let me tell you a little bit about our graduates." They ranged in age from sixteen to eighteen. "Eight states are represented, New York with four, Maryland with two . . ." He thanked the incredible staff and the inspirational faculty for helping bring the children here and out of a darkness that shrouded them when they first came. He thanked the parents again for participating in their own series of therapeutic workbooks, aimed at looping in the parents with their child's own therapy sessions. This attempt at continuity in the therapy was rarely seen by the students. But they didn't care, not the ones sitting up front. At last, they were going home.

"We've tried to roughly figure out the number of hours of therapy you've had," Frank continued, his eyes darting over the graduates and attempting to avoid the student body beyond. "Individually, you've had about three hundred forty hours of individual counseling and somewhere around four thousand hours of group counseling. So you should be awarded an honorary counseling degree for all of that."

The graduates and their parents laughed, though with unease. Someone in the crowd picked their nose. Looking at the eyes of some of the students not graduating, it was possible to see that the whites had turned gray, a bit bloodshot around the edges. A bottle of hand sanitizer mixed with water was shared by all the night before.

Frank blinked over the crowd, sweat in his eyes.

"I received an email recently from someone who graduated from Swift River well over a year ago. And it wasn't a very nice email. In fact, it was a very sad one, because in the email she listed all the people she graduated with who were not doing well. There were a lot. Of course, I couldn't respond to her that, for nearly every student in that group, we had recommended extensions in their programs or recommended programs following that. And she said that, because I was director of counseling at the time, she held me solely accountable for their difficulties. And then she concluded her email with she was doing great, but no thanks to me," he said. The crowd again issued uneasy laughter.

"I couldn't really win. There are a number of things wrong with this email. It was filled with what we therapists call cognitive distortions, or thinking errors."

He called to the graduates, asked them to tell him what they heard in that email that was "inaccurate." It was like therapy. They were being told to think critically of the perceived inaccuracies, never taught to view anything objectively as an individual. They were taught to look at the world through the lens of therapy, identifying problems and never championing successes.

"Lack of responsibility," someone said.

"Blame shifting," another student said.

"Projecting," a third graduate said.

"Oh, now you're really throwing out the terms," Frank continued. "One of the inaccuracies is she gave me a great deal of power," he said, raising his eyebrows in bemusement. "I wish I had that kind of power to change people's lives. And so I thought, what is it that we really do here for students? And I think it comes down to the fact that what we've given you are really the skills to know how to change your own lives, that, when you leave here, all of you know what you need to do to change any aspect of your life. And it's really pretty simple. It's hard to do, but it's really simple. It involves facing one's self, acknowledging there's a problem, finding help, preparing for change, and putting it into action and maintaining it.

"So I feel confident that all our graduates are leaving with a very good toolbox that you can use to apply to your lives now and in the future. Whether you apply those tools is really up to you. And I certainly hope that, if I receive an email from one of you, it will talk about how well you're doing and what you've done with your life since leaving." Frank then walked away from the lectern. Potted plants on the stage fought against a welcome breeze that cooled as fast as it departed.

Avery sat in the crowd, frustrated. She wished she was one of the graduates. They had all reached Level Four and maintained that level for several months, exemplifying the language of the program and also successful home visits, which meant that, when they returned to Swift River, they did not test positive for drugs and their parents reported that their time with their son or daughter was well spent, not disruptive—everything they had hoped they were paying for when they sent their child away. Avery began to cry. She still had many more months at Swift River and, perhaps, more months beyond it, which amounted to unforeseeable years, before she would be on the end of that email Frank mentioned.

A baby cried in the crowd, an unwelcome, cutting, and distant sound that brought her back to realizing there were things outside of her broken, damaged world.

Through Frank's speech, it became clear to Avery that she could not make it "out there" alone. She would need to do her best to learn all she could while at Swift River. She needed to improve her relations with her godmother. She knew that one out of every two hundred students who entered Swift River or similar programs would relapse, making her twenty times more likely to die before turning twenty-nine than any of her peers who had never attended a residential program. The majority of the deaths of former students occurred through accidental poisoning with methadone, heroin, or morphine.

Frank's words about the destiny they chose remained with Avery for the two years she stayed at Swift River. As she built her own therapeutic toolbox, one she believed she could use against the torrid world from which she had come, she listened to Carmen in their individual and group therapy sessions and focused on herself, looking at what caused her to rely on men and realizing she did not need them to feel safe or secure. She looked at her relationship with her godmother and found that it made her angry, so she learned little tricks—controlled breathing, writing in a notebook—to help her through bouts of anger, rather than exploding on the closest person. Locked up at an institution, secluded from the real world and its myriad problems, she could do well. When released back into the wild, she feared finding continued misfortune.

———

"For me, I think ASR [Academy at Swift River] was an awakening," Avery told me. "At the time, it was, I think, where I needed to be. It helped me to understand that just because you've been through fucked-up things in life doesn't make you a fucked-up person. I don't think I could have found the strength in myself to break away from my bad habits without ASR."

She wanted her relationship with her godmother to work. Avery hoped for the best transition possible and applied to the University of Louisiana, where she was accepted. She talked with her godmother in the days leading up to her release, sharing her anxieties, fears, worries, and goals.

As a parting gift, Carmen gave Avery a handwritten card and told her to always shine her light, to never forget the good person she was inside. With the card, Carmen included a pen with the word "Drama" circled and crossed out. She smiled at Avery and said, "Please, no more drama. Promise?" And Avery did, tucking both away into her bag. Carmen also handed Avery a one-page sheet of dos and don'ts for her return home (no smoking, no drinking, no hanging out with her old friends) and a social contract, which reaffirmed the list of dos and don'ts and outlined a curfew and plan for employment and education. She would follow a curfew. She would not go out without her godmother's permission. She would not drink or do drugs and no "partying." In return, her godmother promised to be more forgiving and caring. Everything was set on paper. But life isn't on paper.

Avery went home near the summer of 2009. She hoped to integrate herself back into the family in the way she sought to integrate herself into Swift River's program and philosophy. "You're willing? Then I'm willing. Let's do it," Avery told her godmother when she was picked up at Swift River. She had a graduation like the ones she had attended. She listened to Frank's words, which varied little, hopeful yet concerned. Soon she stepped into a car heading to the airport. Hours later, she arrived in New Orleans and drove with her godmother to their home near Slidell, Louisiana, about forty minutes northeast of New Orleans, as though it were any other day.

Neither Avery nor her godmother found it easy sticking to the case plan or social contract that Carmen had written. Their expectations did not align. Avery figured her godmother might be different and kinder to her after all that she had been through in the last two years. She hoped that her godmother had changed, having said she would do therapeutic work on her own while Avery was away. Her godmother expected that Avery would be more compliant and hoped that she would not revert to her old friendships and boys as crutches. She wanted Avery back in therapy, not because it was on the social contract and case plan but because she wanted to keep an eye on Avery.

For the first few weeks, Avery was not being combative and had found work at a local day care. She spoke her mind but was respectful and did her chores. What more did her godmother want? Still, Avery was sent to another therapist in Harahan, nearly an hour from their home in Slidell and far different than the one she used to visit before being sent away. Since both her godmother and Avery were in therapy, the therapist, Dawn, met with them separately. They talked about their feelings toward one another before the programs, during the programs, and what transpired after. Avery spoke honestly.

"I feel like she's babying me and that she truly doesn't want me in her life," Avery said to Dawn in confidence. "I feel like she doesn't want to be my mother and that I'm just a burden."

"Why is that? She sent you away because she cared about you," Dawn said, sounding to Avery like an agent of her godmother.

"Because it seems like she regrets adopting me. I told my god-mother that I feel like she loves my siblings more than me."

"I think we all need to be honest and share this openly. I'd like to have your godmother come in and hear what you have to say. You need to be honest with her."

"No, you don't understand. She's going to lose her shit. That's not going to work."

At their next session, Avery sat beside her godmother, across from Dawn.

"This is not going to help," Avery said.

"Let's just try," Dawn urged. "Tell her what you told me."

Avery did. "I think you wasted all your savings on Swift River. You don't even stick to your end of the social contract. You treat me like a child. Do you know what I've been through to get this far and still be standing? Do you?"

"It's you who needed the redirection. We were helping you, not the other way around," her godmother said.

"You're a shit-fucking parent," Avery said. "I hate you."

Her godmother got up and left, taking the car and leaving Avery to find a ride home, which took her until later that evening. When she arrived in Slidell, Avery recalled finding that her stuff was packed and sitting in the front yard. "I'm tired of being your bitch all the time" were Avery's last words to her godmother.

She packed her things into a friend's car and drove away.

BOOK III

Lockdown

Mike and Mark

1

It was a blur to me. I just hated the program. I hated the seminars. I remembered there were groups of people, and everybody was in pain because their kids were going through this, so they wanted to get close to you and speak with you as a friend. And I made some friends from the program, still to this day, very close friends actually, but the actual programs themselves and the seminars they made us go through, to me they were torture.

—*Steve, father of Mark and Mike, in an interview*

There were still worse places than home. Mike knew this. Mike went to school one day in 2007 not for class but because Mark, his brother, had fallen into trouble with a group of friends—ripping hood ornaments off priceless cars, smoking marijuana—and as a result had appeared before a juvenile court. One of Mark's friends, already on probation, had begged Mark to take the fall. To help Mark pay for the fine levied by the court, all but one of the kids had pitched in.

That day, Mike went to school to honor his brother and their family name. He was offended that the one teenager who did not pay, Jim, who had been involved with the group of kids but had faced no charges, was not helping Mark pay the fine. During their lunch period, Mike beat Jim brutally and without mercy until the staff and other students pulled him off. Mike was promptly expelled from the school he barely attended, a punishment as inconsequential as a failing grade. Mike was charged with assault at a court hearing attended by his parents. The judge, impressed by the parents' initiative in seeking alternatives that might lead their children away from juvenile detention and incarceration—the legal system writ large—through their discussions with an educational consultant after Mike was expelled, dropped the charges as long as Mike's parents admitted him to a youth program, which he would need to successfully complete before clearing his sentence and the assault and battery charges. He was privileged not because his parents would later find ways to afford other stints in rehabilitation or treatment centers but because the judge sentenced him to a program, a second chance. His parents agreed, with Mike in absentia.

Mike and Mark were in their salad days, on their way to becoming internationally recognized kart racers, when they fell into marijuana dealing and gangland insouciance. In their basement, they had a light tree—red, yellow, green—that allowed them to practice their off-the-line starts. Mike was faster and never let his brother forget it. Mark felt left behind on the track and also at home, where he struggled for the attention of his parents and his brother. The racing was the only way he could have them validate, or evaluate, his existence.

The brothers started racing when they were three years old, riding around dirt tracks on four-wheelers and working their way to racing bigger 50cc dirt bikes by the age of four. Their father, Steve, a general contractor in central New Jersey who landed large county projects, dreamed of traveling abroad for races, staging out of a trailer he bought for his sons. He had raced when he was younger, and he wanted to bring his two young boys into racing in ways he had never had. He never forced them. They raced willingly. "I lived through my kids since the day they were born," Steve said years later. "I always thought to myself, *Geez, if I ever could, I would give my kids an opportunity to race and become professional racers.*"

Racing was the clear focus of their lives, and their grades suffered accordingly. Mark was a slow learner, though he was never formally diagnosed with a learning disability. His teachers viewed him as stupid and lazy, calling him out repeatedly in class. One math teacher, a grumpy woman who seemed frazzled and frustrated every time she spoke to Mark, would berate him for not grasping seemingly simple concepts.

"We went over this last week, don't you remember?"

"I'm trying," he said, staring at the chalkboard while standing in front of the class.

"You need to try harder. I can't believe you're not getting this."

"These all led to reasons why I would fight or skip class," Mark said later. "Why go to class if I can't learn?" He divided his time between racing and video games, a privilege afforded to him by his parents, who seemed to fade from his life the older he got—not from mistreatment or neglect but in the way a boy tends toward growth in his own space and time. "All I knew was means," Mark said almost a decade later. "I didn't know what a struggle was. I was sheltered. But I was also literally the definition of 'emo.' I was always depressed. I was cutting myself, and all I thought about was suicide."

The bond between the brothers also faded. "[Mike] grew into a person way earlier than I did: he was actually into girls way before I was, he was into hanging out with friends. He was into everything way before I was." Mark stayed home, his dirt bike and engine parts in the basement, his gaze affixed to a television screen in his room on which he played Xbox and GameCube. Mark was not just ignoring his family; he felt they were ignoring him.

School only alienated Mark from Mike further still, with Mark trying to keep pace with his brother, like he always had on the racetrack.

Mike seemed to leave Mark behind. "I don't blame him," Mark said. "I was boring, and he saw a cool life."

Mark could not connect with people the way his brother seemed to. Mike had fallen in with a group of guys who skipped school, started fights, and used drugs in between. They were early versions of gangsters, unknowingly grooming themselves for a harder life and indifferent to the consequences. They did not see beyond the conduct of the current hour. Mark was a product of those lost hours. He watched what he believed was the growth of his brother, how he sprouted a set of tough wings and beat them to distinguish himself from their peers. Mark had always been envious of Mike, his ability to breach skyward and chance into groups of friends with little effort.

The boys' parents felt they were under the pressure of time: they only had a few years before the boys would turn eighteen and face real consequences for their actions. Mark and Mike were young— thirteen and fourteen, respectively. Their parents skipped wilderness programs—why they chose a residential program rather than wilderness, the normal trajectory, is not clear—and went straight to programs that would, in due course, they hoped, steer the boys away from the path of criminality.

As their behavior worsened, their father transitioned from a man teaching his sons to race into a man struggling to keep his sons sober and out of prison, working long hours to afford the cost of enrolling each of them into the specialty programs that insurance would not cover. Since the racing ambitions had faded, he dreamed of bringing the boys into the family construction business, which he operated with his brother, a local developer in Monmouth County, New Jersey. "We had a beautiful operation," Steve said of his family business.

Around this time, Steve and his brother began bribing township officials and the local sewer authority to gain favor for their projects. Steve enticed members of the Marlboro Township Planning Board with $4,000 to fund trips to Disney World. By the time agents with the

Federal Bureau of Investigation arrested and charged him early on the morning of December 6, 2006—nearly a year before Mike would be charged with assault—the boys had already begun making inroads into the juvenile criminal justice system.

Steve was charged, along with his brother and a third man, their attorney, with bribery and attempting to obstruct a grand jury investigation. Steve remained out on bail while he waited for the court to take up his case. "For me, it was horrible, because I wasn't able to help them," Steve said years later. "They were going through a horrible situation. My wife was dealing with it on her own." Steve was facing serious prison time as his children spiraled out of control.

He and his wife had to find a way to get their sons help.

A few nights after the judge handed down his sentence for the school-yard fight, Mike was in his bathroom at home, hunched over the toilet in a pubescent curl, thinking of a girl he once dated, when there was a knock on the door. He had known something was coming, a constant anxiety without justification, one he had been able to ignore in part because of the marijuana and carousing. Now he knew what that fear was for.

"Yo, Mike," his father said from outside the bathroom door. "Some people are here to see you."

Mike opened the bathroom door and stepped out.

"These guys are here to take you somewhere," his father said and stepped aside. Behind him were two men aching to get a move on.

"Military school?" Mike asked.

"No," his father said. "It's not military school."

Mike walked over to the dresser in his room and opened the drawer. He stretched on a pair of tight-fitting designer jeans. His hands shook anxiously. He struggled, and when he buttoned the brass above the zipper, Mike reached for a pack of Newport cigarettes and a lighter.

"You're not going to need those where you're going," his father said. Mike remembered thinking the two escorts were weak and fat and lacked intimidation. It hardly mattered. He seemed to quickly become someone he had hidden, a scared young boy unsure of what to do with the feelings coursing through him. "It was almost a relief," Mike said later. "The madness I was creating in my life was over. Something had to give. I didn't fight. I could have easily fought these dudes. I know my neighborhood. I could have gotten out, but I didn't even put up a struggle." This was the peculiar relinquishment of power experienced by the many children escorted before and after Mike, throughout the great saga of the history of tough-love treatment. It was as though they gave in to the transporters not because they had been caught but because they welcomed change and knew, deep down, they needed help.

He went with them willingly, reaching upstate New York after a six-hour drive. When he arrived at the Academy at Ivy Ridge, he was given a cot placed on the hallway floor. The next morning he awakened to screaming, loud shouting, and someone kicking at his cot in the white cinder-block hallway.

"Get out, get out, get up," someone shouted, and children of all ages scrambled from their rooms and lined the walls along the corridor. Kids not much older than Mike were shouting in his face. He thought his father said this *wasn't* a military academy. He stood in the corridor in his boxers; every boy was in his underwear. He was told to place his right hand on the shoulder of the child in front of him, and as a connected single-file line, they marched forward. The clients walked, staying close to the walls as they traversed the corridors and classrooms in otherwise silent lines. Outside the campus walls, nothing but farmland stretched for miles.

On his first day, someone explained to Mike the level system—merit-based levels at which a client is granted simple privileges, like a phone call home—which in every program enforced a false sense of accomplishment and instilled a communal goal, much like a cult. By believing that attaining a higher level made a client better in the eyes of the program, clients had an incentive to lie toward advancement. "It was crazy," Mike said later. When he tried to leave his room to go to the bathroom, he was reprimanded. He needed to ask permission. When he went to ask for permission to go to the bathroom, he looked a counselor in the eyes without first asking permission and was reprimanded again. He looked down at the floor and his shoes the next time he asked. "Can I go sit down?" he asked. The counselor smiled. "Request granted." Mike learned his lesson.

For his intake procedure, Mike was led into a restroom with two men. The restrooms had no partitions, only toilets on the floor. That is where Mike met Jason Finlinson, a large buff man who sipped on small cans of Red Bull, alongside his second-in-command, an equally large and edgy man self-titled the Lieutenant. The Lieutenant drank from a coffee mug filled with beer and smiled between bruised ears, as though he were jumped by thugs before coming into work every day. He told Mike to strip. "You can call me fuck face, douchebag, whatever," the Lieutenant said. "Take everything off. Spread your legs and shake."

"No sweat," Mike said, trying to save face. He was not hiding anything, so he did as he was told. He felt as though he were in a trance, reacting rather than responding, pulled through some unfortunate nightmare over which he had no control. "The truth was, I was in such shock," Mike said later. "I was, like, I want to get a lay of the land before I act out. I don't actually know what is going to be a thing here. I don't know where I am. I don't know who any of these people are. I don't know what country I am in. I don't know anything. I was fully obedient."

Mike went through the motions and crouched in a squatter's stance. He donned the uniform: white underwear, white socks, white button-down dress shirt with a striped red-and-blue tie, a blue sweater vest, khaki pants, patent-leather dress shoes, and a threaded belt that fit all sizes.

Because of Ivy Ridge's religious affiliation, books that were not based on Mormonism were hard to find. Mike was ostracized for being white and Jewish, with a large nose and short black hair, which made him an easy target for the older, more-hardscrabble teens who were there on court orders and not a loose redirection order like his own. He sat before a computer every day after his intake and was told to take lessons, a series of forms that flashed on-screen and that he clicked through toward an unaccredited GED. Between those lessons, there were others: rap groups and shouting matches intended to mimic attack therapy. The staff often gathered the clients, all young boys, in an auditorium and marched them in circles for hours. It was a simple punishment that dissolved any free time the boys might have. Their thoughts were never given time to settle; they were kept constantly on the move and always watching over their shoulders or at the person in front of them, navigating the hallways day and night with their hands on the shoulder ahead of them. "If the person in front tried to run and we don't stop them, we get disciplined," Mike said later.

One day, through a window, he saw a familiar motor home outside the school's gates. It looked like the one Mike's parents owned, the one they used to take to racing events. He swore it was them. "That's my parents," Mike said to the kid behind him.

"Yeah? Maybe they just dropped you here to scare you or something. Can I have all your stuff if you leave?"

"Yeah, whatever, man."

Mike planned to punch the window and make all the noise in the world the moment he saw his parents step out from the motor home. He waited, fighting against his urge to comply, but he wanted to confront them and decided to step free from the line. Boys started shouting and pointing. Another kid shouted, "You are going to get your ass beat. Get back in line, or we'll call it a jailbreak, son."

"A what?" Mike said, only then realizing that the whole auditorium was staring at him and expecting an instructor to tackle him. "Everybody starts freaking out," Mike remembered. But he came to learn there was an incentive to catching runners. The other clients were encouraged to catch the runaway until staff arrived. Oftentimes the runaway was beaten up in the process. The person who caught the runner would get a steak dinner. "There was nowhere safe," Mike said. And when he looked back out the window, the motor home had gone.

It became clear that all rumors came from cliques, which were more like gangs and would become an early lesson for Mike on prison hierarchy. The leader of one group might be working with the Lieutenant or Finlinson, getting in their good graces to help shorten his time until departure, bringing him home sooner. Mike tried to "clique up," but he still fantasized about escape: he noticed there was no barbwire, no fence. But the windows were sealed shut behind metal grates. For more than six months, the entirety of his stay, he remembered breathing fresh air only once. He took to imagining the sun on his skin, the smell of a girl's perfume, hugging himself against the bracing cold of the facility. He lived often in his head, thinking of times and places and people that grew ever more distant the longer he stayed trapped behind the walls of Ivy Ridge.

"One time they took me outside, but everything was a sheet of ice," he said. This breath of fresh air was not a reward. Without any warning, the instructors attacked him, landing hard blows against his body and ripping off his clothes as they went, he said. Vulnerable, exposed not only to the elements and these strange men in upstate New York, Mike curled tight into himself and spun around the ice. He took his licks quietly until they left him to dress alone.

In moments like that, he would return to the past, to better times when he had more control over his life and actions, but he also spent much time looking forward. Planning. Anticipating. He thought a lot about how he would make them pay for what they were doing to him.

He dwelled on how he might get revenge. Another time, as Mike lay in his top bunk reading a book one night, a client named Don rushed in and started beating him, landing punches across Mike's body. In a way, he was suffering the same punishments he had brought on kids and classmates in New Jersey. But he could not imagine deserving it in return. Maybe he did deserve this, he thought, and so he took the beating. Then Don stopped and put on a rubber glove.

"You know what this is for?" Don said and snapped the glove.

"Nah," Mike said.

"Drop your pants," Don said. "It's go time."

"I was, like, 'No,' you know . . . ," Mike said years later. He was saved by a staff member walking through the corridor, conducting a head count before the dormitory lights were turned off. That would not always be the case. Once, when Mike was in the shower, someone approached him from behind and shoved the handle of a broomstick up his rectum. "I didn't cry," he said later. "I didn't want to look weak or anything like that. I never cried, never cried. I never showed weakness, despite how weak I felt, and was, in reality. Today, as a grown man, I am really ashamed of some of the things that happened to me." Mike was thankful that it was just one guy, one broom handle, unlike some of the other clients who received much worse.

His screams were heard by few. Even though Mike could communicate only with his parents through email, the outside world was distant, responses even farther afield. What he did receive in his inbox were messages which ignored his pleas for help. After three months, Mike's parents informed him that they had sent his brother, Mark, to a similar program in Utah. He thought nothing of it and tried to think about what he would say in response, how he might free himself through writing, how he could ever explain the treatment he received. He could not understand why they had ignored his initial plea.

On Sundays, Mike received fifteen minutes of computer time during which he could compose an email home. He felt this treatment—the levels, the shouting, the beatdowns, the broom handle—stepped beyond the conscious bounds of appropriate responses to his own behavior. He tried to summon the words he felt would bring him home. "Dear Mom, Dear Dad," he began. Mike wrote that he was getting beat up every day, that someone had stolen his inhaler, that he was being sexually assaulted. After fifteen minutes, the computer locked and the email was saved. Between that moment and the time they would reach his parents, the emails were often edited by therapists. None of the things he wrote ever reached his parents in full. Even when Mike was able to talk to his parents in person—when they came to visit, days when the campus was manicured and some of the worse clients were hidden in their dormitories, like "what North Korea does when they let the one American journalist come on their grounds," Mike said later—they would not listen. His parents told him that everything he said was exactly what the staff had warned them Mike would say.

More than six months passed, but few things about Mike's behavior changed. For one, he was still angry in his emails home to his parents. He also was not advancing through the levels of the program like other kids. He remained stagnant, disillusioned by even being there. His parents returned to the judge and asked whether he could be transferred to a different program. They felt that nothing about his attitude or disposition had improved during his time at Ivy Ridge. Mike was still the same combative kid they had sent away half a year earlier. He was still writing letters that seemed false and halfhearted, manipulative and exploitative, they said. They told the judge that their other son, Mike's brother, Mark, was at a similar program in Utah and seemingly doing well. They wanted to try sending Mike there. With his gavel, the judge agreed.

"I had told my parents, 'You got to get me out. You don't understand,'" Mike said to me. "Not that they believed anything I said, it was true. I think they saw me not happy. Ivy Ridge emotionally beat me down to just fear and terror, like I was a little child again," he said, "and all I wanted was my mommy and daddy." The manipulative nature of the programs was subtle. His parents were his only source of hope. They were the only ones who could save him from the terrible place they had put him in.

Finlinson heard the news and brought Mike into a room one day, along with two other adult staff members. Mike knew that clients being alone with staff was a nonstarter, meant to protect him from abuse at the hands of staff members. But they were colluding anyway, like that time they stripped him in the field of snow. He felt as if maybe he should have his own client witness too. But this meeting was different. "You're being redirected," Finlinson told him.

As Mike rose from the office chair, he turned to see the escorts, who this time were much larger and foreboding. "They were the real deal," Mike said. They took him in a car and drove him to the airport, where he boarded a flight for the west, somewhere far away. He relived that night he was first taken. It was happening all over again, and this time he had nothing of his own: no jeans, no cigarettes, only the clothes from Ivy Ridge.

On that morning in September 2007 when Mike didn't join Mark and his parents downstairs for breakfast, Steve and his wife told Mark that his brother was sent to a program "to help him get better." Mark shrugged and went about his day, pretending to go to school only to meet up with a friend to smoke marijuana.

"You would think that I would be so heartbroken and I would be, like, 'Mom, where the fuck is Mike?'" Mark said years later. But he wasn't the least bit worried for his brother. "I was, like, 'Sick!' I could smoke all the pot and cigarettes I wanted, because he wouldn't be around to hassle me about it." Mark, now fourteen years old, had recently started at the same high school where Mike had left a pot-connection void for many of his fellow students, and he thought that he could take over Mike's role as dealer. Without his brother, the restraint anchoring him to a quiet life of video games and complacency, Mark let loose.

"Now there is excitement to my life," Mark said. "I am essentially somebody." There were consequences to his getting up every morning, rolling several joints for school, and preparing to sell whatever small bags of leafy green he kept in his backpack. He would be less attentive in class, making him an even easier target for his math teacher. He would focus more on the selling of drugs and the false friendships born of those transactions than on making lasting friends. There were consequences at school, where he would fight whoever irritated him that day, just like his brother had. But he rarely heeded them. He was starting to make friends now that Mike wasn't interfering. People liked him for his drugs, but at least they liked him. He found confidence in the drug game, was more sure-footed in his dealing, which extended and formed his personal life. He didn't care about the choices he made because, for once, they seemed like the right ones: people noticed him, and he was never again alone.

"It was never about consequences," Mark said. "Like, when you are five years old, you don't know that putting your hand in a pit bull's mouth might mean you lose your hand."

Nearly three months after his brother disappeared, on the morning of December 7, 2007, two men appeared in Mark's room to escort him from the house, as they had his brother. "I didn't do anything to resist," Mark said. "I just got up. They said 'put these clothes on' and I said okay." He, like his brother, had never regarded these consequences as threatening and went willingly.

He would not be going to the Academy at Ivy Ridge. It was rare for siblings to exhibit the same character flaws and deranged anger. Even rarer for siblings to attend the same program. Their emotional development and their rehabilitation should be without external influencers. Experts told the parents that each son should do this on his own, and they feared that the boys together in one program might be a toxic combination ripe for failure. Discouraged against sending them both to the same program, they sent Mark across the country to a "reform school" in Utah, where he would spend the next several months at a lockdown facility.

Almost instantly, Mark lost that prideful, articulate, and well-liked veneer he had established after Mike left. He was fond of what he felt he was becoming, but now not a sinew of that former life remained. From the airport, the transporters and Mark reached the school building late in the evening. Located in La Verkin, Utah, the facility known as Cross Creek was a residential treatment center for teenagers four hours south of Salt Lake City, closer to the border with Arizona on a swath of desert in the middle of nowhere. It would be Mark's home for the foreseeable future.

"Peace," the transporters said, before leaving Mark standing at a desk. Behind the desk was a woman dressed in what looked like hospital scrubs. She seemed like a receptionist but spoke with the authority of a headmaster. He turned to the transporters as they left. "Have a nice life," Mark remembered hearing one of the transporters mumble. "Fuckin' kid."

The next few days were filled with rude, intrusive physicals; paperwork; and psych exams, hefty manila envelopes containing things like the Minnesota Multiphasic Personality Inventory (MMPI-A), used to assess major symptoms of social and personal maladjustment. The test had several scales through which patients were measured for their levels of depression, their preoccupation with self-care and health, their need for control or rebellion against control, their inability to trust, and whether or not they had uncommon or odd perceptual experiences. Another test, the Millon Adolescent Clinical Inventory (MACI), which is more specifically for teenagers, measures the emotional patterns and clinical symptoms and teenage apprehensions in juveniles. One hundred and sixty true-or-false questions were aimed to better understand what teens had suffered in their life before the moment when they took the test. But the reliability of the test scores is questionable over long intervals and does not speak for a child as they grow and mature. The MACI only captures a moment in time, nothing systemic. Mark also underwent common IQ testing. All the tests were designed to answer similar questions: Was Mark, at fourteen, destined to be a lifelong addict? Was he on an irreversible path of miscreant behavior, or was there hope yet? Was he bipolar? How lost was he?

Aesthetically, the school felt like an outdated hotel. The walls were all painted white, with ancillary doors leading to other hallways that "went fucking forever. There were tons of doorways. In the middle of the whole building, there is a fence, a shitty, plastic fence. It separated the guys' side and the girls' side."

Staff members had Mark line up against a wall on one of his first days, and he was placed into a group, given a room, and shown where to relieve himself and where he would eat. "I was nervous, real nervous," Mark said later. "I was really self-conscious. I was just standing there. I didn't know what to do." It was as if he'd been sent back in time to the lunchroom to suffer through a lesson he should have learned the first time. "At that point, I was thinking, *I guess this is where I live now. I just wear button-down shirts and khaki pants every day.*"

He spent most of his days under the supervision of a staff member who corralled clients into teams and shuttled them between therapy and classes, marching them like they were military recruits. Many of the rules around when and to whom clients could speak were the same as those at Swift River. Permissions would need to be granted for everything; all decisions were predetermined for the clients by the staff. Later that first week, Mark met the counselor overseeing his case.

"Can I call my mom?" Mark asked, seated across from Boaz, his counselor, in an office of blinding white, like he was staring at the end of his life.

"Nah," Boaz said and sat back in a creaky office chair. "It's the program's policy that clients wait at least a month before speaking to their families."

"A month?"

"It allows you to get . . . settled," Boaz added, struggling for the word.

During those sessions, little happened beyond the occasional mental check-in: "How are you settling in? Fine? Good." In between, Mark would spend hours trying to renew his communication privileges—with his parents, with the other kids—while also skirting his psychiatric therapy aimed at his relationship with his parents. He devised complicated methods of passing notes and messages to other teenagers in the lockup. If he were caught, demerits would keep him in this level for several weeks, prolonging his stay and further preventing contact with his family. When he had to go to the bathroom or cross any threshold, he was required to ask permission, the same way Mike had to ask for permission to sit.

Mark tried making friends when he could, realizing that there was a camaraderie forming in the group since they spent twenty-four hours a day together. He liked a boy named Wilson, who was chill and respectful. They bonded one day when the school gave the boys no more than ten squares of toilet paper for use in the bathroom. Someone had been clogging the toilets, and since it was neither Wilson nor Mark, they forged themselves as a band of brothers against the corporal punishment. They each complained whenever they went to use the restroom, their own small protest. "How am I supposed to wipe with this?" Mark asked the bathroom attendant, who watched the boys through the open stalls as they relieved themselves. "Not my problem," the attendant said. "Blame it on your friends." In such a simple remark came a heavy implication: Indict your friends for their behavior. It is not the school's problem but yours. Take it up with your friends.

That is why Mark had Wilson, someone with whom he could weather the storm and also someone he could trust, despite not knowing much about him. Friendships formed easily in strained environments, everyone looking for something human to attach themselves to. The way the school would turn things onto the clients was a common practice, almost like vigilante justice. The programs aimed to change the way the children saw their world, and it began with degrading their friends, to help them realize the toxic relationships they had at home and now at the program. Most often, the programs, and by extension the staff, focused more heavily on instilling the idea that the clients themselves were the problem, not only for their personal troubles but also for the trouble of their family and friends.

In his first group therapy session, Boaz asked Mark why he thought he was there.

"For fighting," Mark said.

"What about all the drugs you were doing?"

"I don't do drugs," Mark said.

"You don't smoke pot?"

"Yeah, I smoke pot."

"So you're here for pot and fighting. What about disrespect?"

"All right, I think I'm here for that too."

"How about skipping school?"

"Fine, fine, that too," Mark said, feeling that there was no way for him to win against his therapist. It was best to highlight how terrible he was. And he set out to rewrite his story, if only to get off Boaz's radar.

But Mark did not initially feel so terrible. He knew other people were doing worse things and even admitted to them, as happened in a group session later that week.

Near the end of group, a new kid named Teddy was given the same grilling of questions that Mark had had in his first week.

"There is one more thing," Teddy confided to the group. "We had a little toy dog, a lap dog back home named Fufu, and I had sex with her. I lost my virginity to her."

As far as anyone could tell, Teddy was serious. The group exploded.

"No!" boys shouted in unison.

"You fucked your dog?!" another shouted.

"You're a fuckin' rapist, bro," another boy screamed.

Boaz managed to calm the group down, but Teddy was already sobbing and red in the face. Mark was seated nearby. He was there in that group circle because he skipped school and smoked pot, which made him as bad as Teddy. Like revisionist history, the program made people like Mark indict themselves until they believed themselves to be irreversibly bad.

Mark started to obey and asked permission to eat, drink, sit, stand, shit, and sleep. Supervisors and counselors approved his requests, and when he had time to himself, time he had to ask for, Mark—former drug dealer, heavy-hitting fighter—picked up yarn and learned to crochet, something he heard the girls were doing in another part of the building.

Mark shriveled, almost quivering, back into the cherubic little boy who had no friends and spent his days inside. All the insecurities he could not overcome in school flooded back when he arrived at Cross Creek. "Gone," Mark said of his former self. "Disappeared. New person." He felt himself changing as if by force. On the rare occasions when he found himself alone with other clients, he was anxious and eager to break rules, like stealing extra food from the lunch line. But when he was talking to his parents, counselors, or Boaz, he would employ the language of the programs. He used words like "justified" and "rationalized" and terms like "euphoric recall" to describe why he liked drugs. He said of his past behavior that he chose friends who were "toxic and would enable" him to do bad things and that "war storying promoted relapse." He spoke and acted disingenuously, the way he thought everyone wanted him to be.

Four months passed. Another weekly meeting with Boaz—"How are you settling in? Fine? Good."—and more group therapy sessions. Mark was numbing to the idea of Cross Creek, the communal living, the accountability systems, and the levels that he had not managed to ascend. He remained silent for most of his time there, speaking only in group.

"Mark, we have something we've got to tell you," Boaz said in one of their weekly group meetings. Mark knew he was not getting pulled from the program, that his fate was never filled with anything resembling luck. He had not had any contact with his parents and had hardly showed "emotional growth," despite having had a birthday, despite his kowtowing compliance. Now fifteen, he still was unsure of what was happening. The eyes of the group fell on him, making him more squeamish in his plastic seat.

"What is it?" Mark said. Everyone was sitting against the cold, white brick wall, the temperature dropping to near freezing. His blinding anxiety grew.

"Your brother is coming to Cross Creek," Boaz said.

The room held its breath. It was more common for someone to be pulled without warning than it was for their sibling to join them in treatment at reform school.

"Can I talk to him?" Mark asked.

"You cannot talk to him," Boaz said. "We are scared that it would be a risk if you spoke to him. I will figure something out, though, where you could get some time with him initially, but after that you will not be given a chance to speak to or see one another." Mark was in shock. He was excited for the first time since leaving home that fall, since celebrating his birthday alone in a Utah icebox for troubled teens. It had been more than six months since he had seen or spoken to Mike, the time a swirl of routine admonishment. "Oh my God, that's amazing," Mark said.

Chatter broke out among the group: "What?" "Are you serious?" "His brother?" Every once in a while, a brother and a sister might be placed in the school at the same time, but they couldn't talk, write each other letters, nothing, separated always by fifty feet and a flimsy plastic fence halving the building. Genders were already split. The boys never saw the girls and vice versa. A brother and a sister might know of the other's presence but never have an opportunity to meet or chat. But brothers? They would be nearly always in the same arena, within the same building, and visible to one another. They would be presented with opportunities to speak even if they were not allowed to. That was new and worrisome.

In the morning, Boaz brought Mark into a room off the main hallway. Shelves held books and Mormon bibles. A phone sat on the table in front of a small computer screen. Two chairs were set up. Usually in the other chair, Boaz would sit and monitor phone calls, but on this morning, he said, "Just stay here for a minute."

Then, like an apparition, through the doorway stepped Mark's brother, Mike.

2

Some of them would go to jail. And when they're in jail,
you think, *Okay, thank God they're in jail. I want to go visit
my son. He's alive. Thank God.*

—*Steve, father of Mark and Mike, in an interview*

Ivy Ridge and Cross Creek are like many programs catering to
teenager misconduct therapy, more-residential centers that bill
themselves as a preparatory school with a small, innocuous therapeutic component. Economically and philosophically they are similar
to therapeutic boarding schools like Swift River—the brochure pictures
look the same, the tuition is comparable—but in practice and staffing,
the way they execute the therapy is much more drastic and violent.

For onlookers or parents thumbing through a brochure, it is impossible to tell any of these academies apart. Parents find themselves at
bitter ends, forced to trust the educational consultants and high school
administrators to direct them to the program that would suit their child
best. Parents are assured by consultants that there are degrees of therapy
and corrective methods, some more stringent than others. What appears
to be a therapeutic boarding school could very well be the closest thing
to juvenile detention that a child might experience. Whether sentenced

by the courts or sent by their parents, clients were equally likely to end up at either end of the murky spectrum of programs.

A group of parents interested in these therapeutic programs were asked to take an independent survey, according to Professor Michael Gass. The group, divided into those who had enrolled their children and those who had decided against the wilderness and residential track, showed a remarkable difference in outcomes among the children. Fifteen months after the initial call with the consultant, those who were admitted to a program showed few signs of the behavior that got them sent away. Those who instead stayed home and attended regular therapy or community sessions were still "dysfunctional."

But studies like the composite described above, one of dozens conducted in recent years under the direction of Gass and an alliance of wilderness programs known as the Outdoor Behavioral Healthcare Research Cooperative, have been met with skepticism and pushback from health care providers. For one, wilderness treatment is not considered evidence based: there is no consensus among health professionals that wilderness therapy works or is in the least beneficial. And since it does not incorporate any CBT, it is often chided. CBT, the form of psychosocial intervention that focuses on emotional skills to overcome depression and anxiety, used in residential programs, is the benchmark treatment modality of today. However, insurance companies rarely reimburse parents for the programs. Many health insurers cite as reasons for nonreimbursement: facilities in states with lax regulations and oversight, programs that are not accredited, and limited evidence-based therapies such as CBT. Look at where many of the children end up anyway, they say. In 2017, a number of families filed lawsuits in Florida, Kentucky, New York, and Utah against insurers who refused to reimburse them for the wilderness therapy programs to which they sent their children. "The lawsuits . . . were bolstered by federal rules expanding mental health care coverage, and by improvements in the wilderness therapy industry itself," according to a report in the *Boston Globe*. Shortly after the lawsuits were filed, a federal judge in Utah struck down a lawsuit, saying that Aetna, the health care provider, would not be required to cover a member's wilderness therapy treatment.

The lockdown facilities are far worse than wilderness, a residential treatment center, or a therapeutic boarding school—though it's often easier to enroll a client, even without prior wilderness therapy. Remote in their locales and even more distant in their disclosures to parents, they are the last stop before graduation to juvenile detention.

Information in the public record on schools similar to Mike's or Mark's is difficult to find, as few are state certified. Given that the clients are all minors, medical records and inspection reports from agencies such as NATSAP, the National Association of Therapeutic Schools and Programs, are closely guarded for the protection of the juveniles. It is extremely hard to determine much about residential treatment centers like Ivy Ridge. Many simply close and disperse their clients, leaving behind only the allegations from former clients and employees alike. Sometimes, there are lawsuits that offer insight, but when they are settled through out-of-court mediation, the families are paid, and the files are closed and made inaccessible.

In 2005, the Brown Schools filed for bankruptcy, which provided a peek behind the curtain at the business model of lockdown facilities. The company had operated eleven boarding schools and additional education facilities in five states, with $10 million in assets and $50 million in debt. The ongoing and increasing legal battles and settlements facing the Brown Schools, from former clients decrying abuse, were often cited as the main cause of their debt and were mimicked by lawsuits brought against similar programs in the decades after. Meanwhile, a bailout by Universal Health Services, which purchased the Brown Schools' properties for $13.35 million, allowed several of the CEDU-specific facilities to remain open.

The techniques practiced by CEDU, while praised for being a "watered-down" version of Synanon, still incorporated questionable techniques, such as "sleep deprivation" and "confrontational therapy."

Ivy Ridge, operated by the now-defunct World Wide Association of Specialty Programs and Schools (WWASPS), a Utah-based conglomerate of programs for troubled youth, was declared a "boarding school of the future" and had the feeling of a college campus. That's because it once was: a converted college acreage with dorms and steepled brick buildings 128 miles north of Syracuse, New York. The campus placed a façade of prestige over the "prison tier with cells" and the cement-floored walkways on which Mike slept on his first night. The school was similar to Swift River in its offerings: 237 acres for therapy with an educational component that allowed children the ability to attend classes and work toward their high school diploma. Tuition at Ivy Ridge was $3,500 each month, however, while Swift River was closer to $5,000. Sometimes programs like Ivy Ridge were state accredited, enabling them to offer degrees of their own; other times it required close collaboration with a client's former high school to get credits attributed. For clients like Mike, who was not allowed back at his high school, the schooling aimed to prepare him for, at the very least and yet most hopeful, community college after the successful completion of a GED.

Clients at Ivy Ridge had staged a riot in May 2005. Around the evening curfew, at 10:15 p.m., someone pulled the fire alarm. Boys rose from their beds like cellmates. Everyone scattered. Windows were smashed and furniture overturned. Other clients tried to help the older faculty wrangle some of the kids, knowing well that if they helped, their stay at Ivy Ridge might be truncated. Eleven of the most ambitious clients ran toward the Canadian border. Into the crisp, warm spring air they fled, but soon they were caught by US Border Patrol agents, county sheriff deputies, state troopers, and Ogdensburg police officers. Twelve clients were arrested. Forty-eight clients were expelled from the school.

Jason Finlinson, who was then thirty-three years old and the director of Ivy Ridge, would later blame the eruption on the children, stating that the melee was in fact what happened with teenagers who run wild in an environment of intense rehabilitation. He said it had little to do with the academy or its code of conduct. He assured the national and local press that the worst clients, the orchestrators behind the riot, had been removed.

The New York State attorney general at the time, Eliot Spitzer, was already investigating the academic accreditation of the school, which offered clients a New York State diploma. Meanwhile, state police were investigating allegations of child neglect and abuse. "We're in a pretty controversial industry," Finlinson said at the time. "When you're trying to change people's lives, there's controversy. If I didn't want the controversy, I'd go wash cars."

In August of that year, Ivy Ridge was forced to refund more than $1 million in tuition money to parents for "grossly misrepresenting its academic credentials." It had awarded diplomas to 113 clients without the authority to do so. "It is a behavior modification center," a state Department of Education spokesperson said at the time, "not a school." The cursory acknowledgment of such a place was unsettling but quickly glossed over. The news led parents and childcare advocates to note that allegations of abuse continued no matter where they placed their sons and daughters, though no criminal charges had ever been brought. Finlinson stood by his staff and team, disregarding the failure to provide accredited education. "We go to great lengths to make sure it's a safe environment," he said. He touted the cameras around the school. He pointed to a rule that prohibited one-on-one interactions between adults and clients, which was why he had been standing there alongside the Lieutenant for Mike's strip-down.

The Academy at Ivy Ridge would close in 2009, after allegations of false imprisonment, child abuse, and gross negligence roiled the school. Families filed class-action lawsuits against the staff and the program in the years after the New York State attorney general ordered the program to stop its issuance of fake high school diplomas. The attorney general also demanded that the school stop advertising itself as an accredited high school.

From the survivor groups online and investigations by state police, stories of abuse, neglect, discomfort, and destitution became public as former clients aged into adulthood. They spoke out about how revealing a thought of sex might lead them to a punishment in the form of writing a ten-thousand-word essay about sexual deviance. They spoke of sexual conversion therapies. At another program, clients were oversedated with medications when they refused to follow staff demands. In a program in Maine, smiling without permission led to toilet duty, for which they were given only a toothbrush. In Florida, a state that bans the inspection of evidence-based treatment facilities, there have been more than 160 allegations of abuse in similar programs. At least ninety kids have died in programs since the early 1990s, with as many as ten at one program in New Mexico. In Costa Rica, a program director was arrested on charges of physical and psychological mistreatment of children but never formally charged.

His name was Jason Finlinson.

———

Cross Creek was likewise operated by the WWASPS, the conglomerate of programs for troubled youth. The nonprofit organization helmed by Ken Kay, the organization's president, hired Robert Lichfield to oversee Cross Creek. Lichfield had experience overseeing the Provo Canyon Boys School, a residential program shuttered in the 1970s by the state of Utah for abuse and maltreatment of clients. (The program has since reopened.) The WWASPS was founded in 1998 and aimed to learn from what Provo Canyon had done in the way of reforming self-destructing teens.

Cross Creek, whose motto was "Not just a program, but a solu-tion," and Ivy Ridge differentiated themselves from Swift River and wilderness programs by their more-stringent and oftentimes religion-based approach to therapy. Rather than modifying methods of therapy known to work on adults, the lockdown facilities used corporal punish-ment and physical abuse to reshape behavior. Clients could be placed into solitary confinement or have their limbs bound to prevent move-ment. More like drill instructors than therapists or counselors, staff used shouting and yelling and threats of physical violence to keep clients obedient. Many former clients told me that sedatives were given at one program, Island View, to quell client disobedience.

Annual tuition at Cross Creek cost parents more than $50,000, not including a $2,000 processing fee and roughly $100 each month toward clothing and sundries for their child. WWASPS offered prorated tuition for any parent who gave the school a referral.

By 2003, Kay and the nonprofit oversaw nine boarding schools. In May of that year, Lichfield was jailed for his mismanagement of a spin-off program in Costa Rica called Academy at Dundee Ranch, oper-ated by Jason Finlinson and similar to the WWASPS program Morava Academy, which operated out of the Czech Republic and was closed for widespread physical abuse. (Another program, Paradise Cove in Samoa, was likewise closed.) The programs that were born of Swift River and similar idyllic, exotic locales and centers were then being sued for false imprisonment, misrepresentation, and concealment. Whereas program brochures touted smiling teenagers and percentages for college place-ment of graduating seniors, the truth on the inside was much more harrowing. Soon lawsuits were filed against WWASPS for child abuse, fraud, breach of contract, conspiracy, gross negligence, RICO viola-tions, false imprisonment, assault, battery, and more.

An attorney in California who helped bring the lawsuits against WWASPS in 2006, Thomas Burton, told local Utah media at the time, "These are not the same kind of cases where someone dies of dehydration or commits suicide by jumping off a cliff. Here the injuries are more psychological than physical. Here the primary physical injury is being locked up against your will when you haven't done anything wrong, someone doesn't like your lifestyle or your friends."

The crux of the boarding schools and residential facilities—and, in part, wilderness therapy—was the stages of group development: forming, storming, norming, and performing. The idea was that a group would come together, argue, then achieve a normal routine and start acting it out in a sort of faux performance. The theory was coined in 1965 by Bruce Tuckman, a theorist in group dynamics. The group dynamic systems meant that children entering the programs were not meant to be pliable at first; rather, they lived up to the reasons they were there by at first receding into quiet, individual, or bombastic states, anything that might alienate them from the larger group (e.g., Libby, the girl who stabbed herself with a stick in Hazel's program, or the dark-blue coat kid from Avery's program). In the second phase, infighting or sorting occurs, when the group begins to assimilate to its environment or trust one another more. How the "storms" manifest (wrist slitting, truth lists, verbal hazing), and their duration (six months, eighteen months) varies between groups. Others might skip to the third stage of group development, in which the group members are cooperative among themselves and with their environment. The tolerance of others and those within the group is an accepted norm. One of the cautions about this stage is that a reluctance is born of the norm: a reluctance to fight or spark conflict—which could often be seen as the sharing of ideas no longer being encouraged—like the ambivalence with which a child goes along with intimidating transporters who arrive at dawn.

Such institutions and their sociobehavioral dichotomies sit atop a long history of social improvement and educational innovations, where upper-scale public boarding schools brought virtue and honor to the children who attended them. In the 1850s through the 1930s, many of those schools were emulated as institutions for released prisoners or felons, the elderly, the disabled, and war veterans and as schools for children with disabilities or mental health problems: what worked for the fortunate may also work for others.

Asylums, as they were earlier called, aimed at the treatment of developmentally or mentally ill patients of all ages; now called psychiatric hospitals or wards, they have a stigma that follows patients for the rest of their lives, limiting things like gun ownership and employment. They are seen in today's society as indicative of someone who is loony and unfit for participation in society writ large. The US Supreme Court went as far as declaring it a violation of basic civil liberties and human rights to be sequestered at a program against one's will and for indefinite periods if the person was not deemed to be a danger to themselves or others. Those admitted to tough-love programs have no such protections. They face no outward stigma and do not receive veritable black marks on their records. They skirt a system meant to stymie the growth of criminality. Rather than suppress criminality involuntarily and momentarily, the troubled-teen programs birth it.

In the vein of Bruce Tuckman's stages of group development—form, storm, norm, perform—the girls went one way and the boys went another. Whereas Hazel and Avery went home to face the storming before norming again, both of them falling out with their guardians, Mike and Mark played into the system. They learned and internalized practices suited for institutions but not the world outside those walls. The brothers succumbed to the social phenomenon of the programs and became their own worst champions, assimilating so well that they would face mounting difficulties upon reentry to society.

3

We felt at ease because we knew that there was a pause on this crazy lifestyle they were living, similar to when you go to jail.

—*Steve, father of Mark and Mike, in an interview*

Mike arrived in La Verkin fresh from Ivy Ridge, changed but still recognizable to his younger brother, Mark. The changes were subtle, subsurface. He was more cautious, stiffened by the regiment of programs and the intake sequence he knew better than anything else in his short life: the physical exam, the catcher's stance, the cupping of his scrotum and the coughing, the intrusive questions, the drab clothing, and the initiation of meeting a new cast of disreputables.

The odd comfort they found in the routine of the onboarding intake was a paramount part of the experience for Mark and Mike, and for the other children swept through the system. Parents placed their hopes for behavior change in the facility's much-touted redirection treatment—a process by which a therapist or counselor redirects or refocuses a client's behavior, attention, or thought processes from maladaptive thoughts or behaviors to more-adaptive ones. This can be achieved through several techniques, including cognitive restructuring, challenging maladaptive thinking, disputing beliefs, and learning new coping skills, according to the *Encyclopedia of Clinical Neuropsychology*. Redirection treatment aimed to prevent clients' initiation into the juvenile justice system, often seen as a pipeline for adult prisons and long-term incarceration, as a springboard to adulthood. Yet the experience of strict therapeutic institutionalization—rural and isolated locations with restricted personal liberties, uniforms, rules and codes of conduct reliant on hierarchical management systems, the rigid separation of the sexes—groomed them to feel more at home in institutions than in their families.

When he arrived at the Cross Creek facility and after finishing the intake procedures, Mike was led to a small room. Inside he found his brother seated at a table, with chairs fanned around a computer monitor and a phone. When Mark saw Mike enter, he stood up.

"I will give you five minutes," Boaz said, leaving the room with the door cracked slightly ajar. ("Something quick, which was terrible, but it was something," Mark remembered later.) The brothers hugged. It was the first time Mark had felt warm in months.

"How are you?" Mark asked.

"How are *you*?" Mike replied.

Mike remembered his brother as he always had: standoffish, dorky, and a bit nervous. For a moment, he saw in Mark's face the little brother with whom he once raced dirt bikes. "For a split second, I saw this authentic, genuine happiness to see me," Mike said years later. "His stupid, ugly smile. I was so thrilled to see my brother. Anything else did not matter." Then the love, like any moment, vanished, and they were back at a program, down to the business of sorting out the hierarchy of the setup and the ins and outs of what could be circumvented.

"Why did you get in trouble as soon as I left, bro?" Mike asked. "You should have stayed good. You saw what Mom and Dad did to me; couldn't you see that this was going to happen to you?"

"I don't know, man," Mark said. "Whatever."

"They will do this to us," Mike said, looking around the small room. He was trying to prove a point that his brother should have listened to him because now they were both in trouble, in a program somewhere without the slightest hint toward their future. "So, like, what's the deal here? Give me the skinny."

"Well, there's softball on Tuesday," Mark began. "Once in a while, we get to talk to each other, I guess." Mark thought for a second. "Food's 'ight."

"No, man, who is the big dog? Who do I got to know in here?"

"I don't know, bro, probably the therapist? His name is Boaz, you just met him. He's a pretty big dude, I guess."

Mike wanted Mark to snap out of the haze, to see the situation he was in. He wanted his brother to help him learn how to manipulate the levels and who the key players were, not when the extracurricular activities were held. Mike worried that the program had made his brother lame and soft and that this facility would be worse than Ivy Ridge. For what he saw in front of him, he also felt sad. Mark had lived up to Mike's image, and in a way, though Mark was still softer and lamer than himself, Mike felt he had let his little brother down.

"He just wanted to be like me. I thought I was cool. The image I had of myself was good. He wanted to be like me. He wanted to do what I did, dress like me, whatever, but he wasn't like that when I seen him," Mike said later. His brother had changed, but beneath it, he could still see his small, scared little brother from the racetracks.

Boaz entered the room.

"That's it," Boaz said, another staff member at his side. "Here's the rundown, as, Mark, you already know. You can't talk to each other. You can't acknowledge that the other person exists. That goes for anyone, Mike. Not just your brother. There are four levels . . ." Mike knew none of this mattered. He listened with a calloused stare, a cold indifference.

Back home, their father, Steve, entered a guilty plea in October 2007, before his brother and their coconspirator were sentenced and locked away in prison. As he awaited sentencing, he alternately worried about his future and that of his sons. This would lead to a reprieve from lockdown for Mike and Mark. Their mother arrived within the first two weeks of September 2008 to grab the boys from Cross Creek while their father was still free on bail, before his sentencing hearing.

"My mom and Mike got in the car, and he turned the volume all the way up, all four doors open, and blasted some rap," Mark said later.

"What are you doing?" Mark and his mother shouted.

"I am just letting the people know that we are outa here," Mike said.

In less than eight months, in March 2009, Steve would be sentenced to thirty months in federal prison. The brothers had known that their father was entangled in a legal battle but were uncertain about the details. Mark remembered Mike was so nervous that he defecated in his pants while on the airplane back to New Jersey. When they got home, Mike was almost seventeen years old, and Mark would turn sixteen later that year, each on the precipice of adulthood, which for them didn't mean college but adult court and hard time like their father. They sat with their parents and talked to both of them, urging them and pleading. They argued that what they were doing before being sent away was not all that bad, that they were under control.

"They always tell us, 'We did what we thought would save your life,'" Mark said later. "I said, 'Listen, all I did was smoke pot.'"

Marijuana as a substance is controversial, often cited as a "gateway drug." Although some studies have found a correlation between early marijuana use and the development of a substance-use disorder, "the majority of people who use marijuana do not go on to use other, 'harder' substances," according to the National Institute on Drug Abuse.

The use of harder substances is strongly linked to teens battling depression, anxiety, and mood disorders. The rate of adolescents aged twelve to seventeen who report symptoms consistent with major depression rose 52 percent from 2005 to 2017. In young adults aged eighteen to twenty-five, that rate increased 63 percent from 2009 to 2017. Linked to this troubling trend are the amount of screen time on mobile devices that teens get and a lack of sufficient sleep. According to clinical psychologist Aaron Fobian, "Teenagers definitely use social media in a way that affects their sleep. It also affects their social interactions with others . . . Spending time with people face to face is a big protective factor against depression." Environment and socialization still make up a large part of addiction risk, but there is a genetic component to both mental health disorders and addiction that makes for unfavorable odds once a child begins to develop a disorder.

The correlation between drug use and depression in teens is clear: 31 percent of teens who experienced depression had used illicit drugs in the previous year, according to a 2015 national survey. The proportion of teens who used illicit drugs but did not have depression was only 17 percent. There is no way to prove whether drug use causes depression or vice versa, but some see this correlation as an indication that teens are self-medicating. Once teens begin using drugs to treat mental illness, they run the risk of developing substance-use disorders. This adds addiction to the list of illnesses they need to manage simultaneously, what are known as co-occurring disorders.

The situation only gets more difficult from an interventionist standpoint. When a patient goes into treatment for a substance-use disorder but a mental illness is left undiagnosed or untreated, substance-use treatment is less successful. Conversely, solely treating the mental illness for which a patient was trying to self-medicate will not make any subsequent substance abuse disappear.

The National Institute on Drug Abuse notes that the largest proportion of adolescents who receive treatment for a substance-use disorder are referred by the juvenile justice system. One possible interpretation of that statistic is that the justice system is favoring rehabilitation over incarceration for young Americans, to avoid the consequences and harms of housing youths in adult prisons. Another interpretation of that statistic is that many young men and women in the United States are going untreated for their addictions or mood disorders. In a survey of ten thousand American teenagers, conducted by Duke University, "more than half of adolescents with psychiatric disorders receive no treatment of any sort."

Those who receive treatment often do so from someone who is not a mental health specialist. This offers little hope to the diagnosed and undiagnosed alike. When mental health issues are neglected or inadequately treated, a possible outcome is death by suicide, whether it be intentional or is pursued through other provocations and life choices.

Mike followed this general progression when he returned home, wanting to get back into drugs harder than before. He tried LSD and hallucinogenic mushrooms, while also smoking more pot than ever. He tried crack cocaine with his rowdy group of friends and promptly became addicted. Soon after, he was charged with driving under the influence and jailed for several days.

When Mark next saw his brother, at a party in central New Jersey, Mike was no longer himself. His eyes were wide, his actions furious, his grip on himself lost. Mike grabbed a glass bottle of vodka and stormed off elsewhere at the party, intending to jump a teenager named John. Mark ignored it until a mutual friend approached him, worried and out of breath.

"Yo, your brother's about to kill this kid," the friend told Mark. He raced to find his brother, who was with three other friends at the far end of the lawn outside the party.

"I'm going to fucking kill this kid," Mike told his friends as Mark approached.

"No, no, no, you can't," Mark said and grabbed his brother, trying to restrain him. Mark believed he was the only person who could control his brother. He also knew that Mike would never hurt him, at least not on purpose. As Mark yelled and shouted and held his brother, Mike struggled to free himself—what seemed to both a recurring theme.

"Mark," he said. "Let me go. I'm not going to hurt you, but let me go."

The anger seemed to settle, and Mike calmed down. Mark began to walk away, and everything seemed quiet, if disorderly. Then Mike took off, reached John, and his fists came down like a hailstorm. A riot flared. Punches and drinks flew. Mark took a hit to the jaw from someone he could not see. Everything appeared to be in slow motion, while happening at top speed. Mike and his friends bore down on John, working toward carrying out his promise to kill. They towered over John as he crumpled beneath their blows. It was not a fight but, rather, a beatdown. Then off the porch a metal patio chair came flying and hit John in the face, below the eye, and his jaw snapped loose from his face.

The group scattered when the police arrived, and the party was no more. Mark and Mike fled in different directions. "I just wanted to keep running away, and I didn't know what I was running from, but it really was just myself," Mike said years later. "I was so emotional and so lost in life: *This isn't working, it must be Jersey. I gotta run.*"

During a family visit to the federal prison in West Virginia, Steve learned that the cops were looking to charge Mike with assault from the fight at the party and that, when he turned eighteen, the court would sentence him as an adult. His guilt was never in question. The family thought of ways to keep him safe and out of trouble. Rather than letting him do his time, someone suggested he go live with family in Israel. Wanting to be with his brother, Mark followed Mike overseas. Though it delayed prison time for Mike, the trip would further exacerbate the pair's self-destruction.

When the brothers returned home to New Jersey, after the money ran out, Mike was sentenced for the battery and assault and served concurrent time for one of his DUIs. Mike likened Ivy Ridge and Cross Creek to the way he felt in jail. "I would say it's the same. It's more like you're building energy. As soon as you get out, everything is the same. Our behavior is the same, our mentality is the same, but our resources are infinite." In jail, Mike met Dempsey, who went by his street name, "CK." He was in for a litany of drug charges, and they immediately hit it off. They shared a cell for that one year until Mike was released, all the while "planning how we were going to take over the world when we got out."

When released, Mike moved back into his parents' house. He was now an adult with a felony record. In a way, he had graduated, but not in the way his family had hoped.

"It was a year, but unfortunately a year wasn't enough," Steve said later of his sons' time in tough love. "You needed ten years, and we ran out of money way before then. They came out of these programs and they would become adults . . . The expectation at that point, when you get kids like that—you're not worrying about what they're going to do with their lives, you're worrying if they're going to have a life."

At least on this Mike and his father agreed. "I had the disease of addiction," Mike said years later. "I'm not a smart guy. I just know I had this feeling of impending doom all the time. My life was based on fear. Honestly, what happened up to that point is nothing compared to what happened after."

———

While Mike did not return to youth lockdown, instead quickly trading up for the real thing, Mark was destined for one more stint at a different—but very similar—facility. Back at his parents' house, he became the kid siphoning his family's wares toward a growing affliction. It was the winter before he turned seventeen, which seemed a long few months away, and eighteen seemed even further—like it would never come. His parents still believed there was hope for him, unlike for Mike, who had gone too deep and had become almost irretrievable.

Since returning home from Cross Creek, Mark had not gone back to high school. He dropped out and began working for his father's construction company, but after three weeks, the work bored him. He returned to school, where he fell back into the same routine of truancy and drugs, seeking approbation. He wanted, like Hazel and Avery, to be "normal." They each fought against a deep insecurity and insufficiency that, throughout their time in treatment, was never addressed. They donned personas that never quite fit. When Mark went back to school, he looked out at a sea of children and found he had no place among them. He had alienated himself. Now he ostracized himself from the school.

He remembered delivering his dad to prison, which was a difficult subject to broach at school. How was he to explain to classmates that, no, his dad was not a criminal but that he did something wrong and would be gone for a short while? Was that not the same thing as a felon? Was that not someone to stay away from? How was he supposed to explain his disappointments? How could he relate to his classmates, who did not suffer from constant therapy, the institutional experiences he had? What did they know about kidnapping? He preferred not to have those discussions. He preferred to avoid people altogether.

Mark had always been a "very 'good child'" compared to his brother. "He told me to do as he said and not as he did," Mark said. That much he remembered "before I ever got into drugs or got into alcohol or became rude or disrespectful." Mike used to be against drugs, used to think drugs were bad. Mark, like his brother, had acquired a few friends since coming home from Cross Creek, but they had less than ideal after-school hobbies. "I think, over time, things just dissipated, and drugs weren't so bad anymore," he said years later.

Their parents had little control of Mike now and watched him drift into legal adulthood, legal and adult consequences. Mark, though, was underage, and although Mike might not be savable, Mark still had time to learn before his eighteenth birthday.

So one morning, Mark awoke to the sight of two men standing in his bedroom doorway. Mark rubbed the sleep from his eyes and saw the two transporters toss him a shirt.

"Are these the pants you wore yesterday?" one of the men said.

"Yeah," Mark said and stood up, pulling the shirt over his head.

"All right, I ran the pockets already. They're empty. Put 'em on."

Mark put on his pants, and the trio sped to the airport.

Ambivalence in adolescence is a dangerous affliction, and this feeling embraced Mark as he watched a series of cabins on a ranch come into sharper focus along the horizon. Sending Mark away again was the geographic cure that Hazel's mother, Paula, had sought—shunting from one program to the next, hoping a new set of circumstances, a new group of people, could bring about change to a person whose desires remained unchanged.

Since their return, the brothers' mother had been struggling to find the right schools and programs for them, despite all the advice given to her by the educational consultants and therapists at Cross Creek. But beyond the daily or weekly therapy given at these programs, she was at a loss for finding a concrete plan to save her boys. What the educational consultants and the school administrators perhaps did not tell the brothers' parents was that Mike and Mark were the rule rather than the exception for what becomes of kids after leaving these programs. The National Institute on Drug Abuse reported that 58 percent of high school students will try alcohol by their senior year. Fifty percent will have "taken an illegal drug" such as marijuana, roughly 25 percent will have smoked a cigarette (all grades in high school showed a "substantial and significant increase in vaping"), and over 20 percent will have "used a prescription drug for a nonmedical reason." Mark and Mike, by all statistical analyses, were in good and growing company.

The snow along the road into the ranch rose four feet high. The wooden cabins and the ranch houses, the barns and the stables, were dusted by a recent snowfall. The ranch was remote and silent, the quietest environment Mark had ever experienced. It made his thoughts run wild. As far as he knew, all such programs were in Utah. This one was called Sorenson's Ranch, and it had yet another set of levels and rules.

He was comforted by the order of the intake: He felt less alone, less isolated by the prospect that he would be frisked and searched and, in those first few hours, would become the object of obsession and curiosity for everyone at the program. He was the center of attention again. He knew how things worked. He could be envied and admired by the others. Soon he was. "I get there, and I stay by myself. I don't know the situation. It's guys and girls mixed this time, not in the same room but you hang out with the girls, which is beautiful," Mark said years later. At Cross Creek, "you couldn't even look at a girl for longer than three seconds. Now I can hang out with them, sit on a couch with them. I loved it." The programs, he was aware then, were trying to instill normal behaviors. He knew that Cross Creek had tried to set up clients with a healthy routine, to teach them to become a well-adjusted adult and to dress right, respect one's self.

"The second program," he said, referring to Sorenson's Ranch, "they didn't teach us anything. There was no therapy." The school's website states, "Our contingency-based behavior modification approach provides consistent and predictable consequences for behaviors. Over time, this helps the student make the connection between action and consequences. This is the foundation necessary for taking personal responsibility, not only for behaviors, but also for emotions and attitudes." It adds, "We don't offer a 'quick fix,' but we do change behavior and habits." Mark was changed by his experience there, not only because the program's inmates, as he had begun calling them, were worse but because the program's structure was not much different from Cross Creek. There were horses and barns and desert landscapes stretching for miles, but the system of arbitrary levels, which he would climb only to gain small privileges like a call home, didn't goad him into buying the program's ethos. He knew already how to navigate such a program. All he had to do was lie, and by giving counselors and instructors the lip service they required, that of a compliant individual using the phony language of therapy, he could sneak off and huff paint or plan a great escape. It broke Mark into two: the person his parents wanted him to be against the person Mark was learning to be in order to survive.

For the first week, they took away Mark's shoes, so he could not run, and paired him with a peer who would be with him always. Then they shaved his head, a first for him throughout his time in these programs but not uncommon in prison, taking with his hair and shoes his sense of self and identity. He had been through this before, a veteran of the industry, and knew to keep busy and out of trouble until he was moved up the levels to a place of more freedom. This came quick for him. He watched with subtle amusement the other clients who were in solitary confinement in an isolation cabin for fifteen hours each day. He watched as boys were made to "hold the wall": disruptive inmates were made to sit against the wall as if in an invisible chair until their legs began to shake. He worked alongside young boys and girls who shoveled horse manure and dug holes that were filled with the dirt they had excavated hours before, moving on to another hole shortly after.

Many former clients of Sorenson's Ranch still allege widespread child abuse that went unchecked by lax laws, and generous kick- backs provided to politicians from the school's exorbitant tuition. The Sorensons were also litigious. They threatened lawsuits against survi- vors who posted negative testimonial accounts on social media. Despite such threats, the accounts of abuse have continued to proliferate. Yet Sorenson's Ranch remains open.

At the ranch, Mark adopted a tougher, carefree air. He was grow- ing like his brother had at the programs: stiff and sure-footed, unafraid and less awkward, self-sufficient in their loneliness. One day, after Mark had been there for three weeks, friendless and brooding, three boys approached him as he sat on the couch in the ranch. Standing at the foot of the couch were Dylan, Jessie, and Darrius, from Alaska, California, and Washington, DC, respectively. Mark was familiar with Dylan and Jessie, who had been there a few weeks as well and who seemed like surfer boys, with wavy, ruffled mops of blond hair. Darrius was a new kid, with short hair and sleepy eyes. Mark did not trust his eyes, hated his face, just because.

"You want to come talk to us?" Dylan said.

"All right, I'll come hang out with you," Mark said. Like high school, he had no friends here. But unlike high school, other clients were approaching him. He wanted to sit with the boys who were liked, and these were those boys. They gathered around a table and sat in seats, like an interview, Mark at the arc of a crescent facing the other three.

"You don't seem like a snitch," Jessie said.

"I'm not," Mark said.

"You want to run with us?" Darrius asked.

"Yeah." Mark had seen several attempts of people trying to run away from the ranch. They were hours from any city, but still they tried. One of the three boys had hatched a plan and briefed Mark. They needed more bodies to help subdue the guards, and once outside, they could pool resources and contacts on their way to Salt Lake City. They cared very little about Mark otherwise.

"There are two night staff, right? One for the girls and one for us," Jessie said. "When Mac comes and walks upstairs to one of the cabins, we're gonna jump him." The boys planned to immobilize the guard, hog-tie him, then steal his station wagon and throw him in the trunk. From there they would drive the four hours southwest toward Las Vegas, abandoning Mac—still hog-tied and unconscious—in a snowdrift along the highway, where he would likely freeze to death.

"We never thought past Vegas," Mark told me. He agreed to their plan, and later that night, they decided it was time to go. Mark began to think about the consequences as he crept toward the cabin where Mac was making his evening rounds, but peer pressure won out. He wanted a reason to bail, one that would not make him look like a snitch or a loser. His new friends depended on him, and he did not want to let them down.

Mark carried a skateboard. He prowled up the stairs, followed by Dylan. Mac entered a room at the end of the hallway, and the boys crouched outside the doorway to the room where the guard stayed. Mark raised the board above his head, prepared to strike. He and the other boys traded worried glances. Reality struck. "Actually having to kill someone," Mark reflected and trailed off. "I wasn't with it anymore." Mark ran down the stairs and the boys followed. They disappeared into their rooms and hid under their blankets, pretending to sleep until morning, worried that someone might have heard them scurrying about.

The program directors learned about the plan a few days later. Someone had snitched, and the kids at the ranch thought it was Mark. He went back to sitting alone on the couch, under heightened supervision. Instead of being flanked by his friends, he was surrounded by staff members who watched his every move. He celebrated his seventeenth birthday under watch, without anyone to wish him well.

Mark spent his final month at the ranch secretly huffing gas in a field and hatching more plans to run and fight and steal, but alone in his head and not with the help of others. He was entering adulthood, and yet he was stuck in a cycle of adolescent mistakes and punishment. He would be released from Sorenson's Ranch with no more skills or knowledge about how to function in the world than when he entered.

"Being a kid was all I knew."

BOOK IV

Afterlife; or,

For Forever

1

The Programs Today

Nothing about my story, nothing about my life, nothing is normal," Avery told me years later. "I've never just had the same things as other kids. It's like, why can't I be a normal kid? Why can't I be a normal person?"

Avery kept in touch with many people from Swift River. In that Facebook group, people often posted about the lives that befell them afterward. Some blamed the programs. Others said that it was bad luck. Still fewer blamed themselves. Over the next decade, Liam, the young boy who castigated Avery in the group therapy session, and even Tom, the cherubic boy at graduation who chewed his gum, died. Others vanished.

Tyler, thirty-two, suicide by hanging; Alden, twenty-three, suicide by self-inflicted gunshot; William, twenty-six, stroke induced by heart failure, attributed to years of intravenous opiate use; Michael, twenty-five, fentanyl overdose; Paul, twenty-eight, accidental heroin overdose; Samuel, twenty-three, intentional prescription pill overdose; Abbey, twenty-seven, a single mother, suicide by jumping onto an interstate highway. Not included in this list are the young man who was shot and killed in an otherwise charming suburb of Chicago or those incarcerated or released on parole for drug possession and distribution.

Gatherings of former graduates proliferated on social media. Some were hidden, and most were private. They acted bilaterally as support groups for those who felt mistreated and as places where former clients went to voice their desire to shut these programs down or to mourn someone they had met at a program who had then been lost. They said that their experiences scarred them emotionally, that they were physically abused.

Some who have left these programs and traversed into adulthood remain in a state of constant flux, like they cannot escape their adolescence. They were tested repeatedly as children, reduced to shells of their former selves with the promise of being built up, better and more whole. Despite efforts to piece themselves back together, many remain fractured, never quite as strong in the places that had been broken. With no evidence beyond anecdotal testimony and the subjective nature of emotional abuse, former students find themselves questioning their experience—and a cycle of self-loathing and guilt continues.

When I shared the amount of people I knew from the programs who were dying from suicide, drug overdose, or murder with Lauren-Brooke Eisen, then senior counsel at the Brennan Center for Justice and the author of *Inside Private Prisons: An American Dilemma in the Age of Mass Incarceration*, she said, "Those are staggeringly high numbers."

"It's concerning," said Dr. Kristin Holland, the lead behavioral scientist at the Centers for Disease Control and Prevention. "I assume that people who have gone to those facilities face stigma in their communities and society in general. We would imagine that students who attend a boarding school like that would be at higher risk for suicide and accidental overdose." As one industry professional told me, responses to the deaths of teens who attended these programs disappear in one simple sentence: "We tried our best, but they were too fucked up."

As a reporter and a human, I wanted to learn more about the correlation between our time in these programs and the deaths of so many of my former classmates, which also made me ask: How are some of us still alive? It had been ten years since I had left my last program, though only five if you counted my final stint in jail. What I learned through my reporting is just how few people have let go of those years and their experiences in treatment. They harbor a burning hatred for those programs. Others pretend nothing happened, which makes it easier to live and work among people who never experienced the programs. Still more cannot explain why they have always been failures, why they can never satisfy their parents, why they could not finish school and languish in dead-end jobs.

Jeremy, whom I met at Aspen Ranch in Utah, told me how one night, in his early twenties, he shared heroin with his friend and then went home. In the morning, he would learn his friend had died from an overdose, and he was nearly charged with his friend's murder. Jeremy now operates a sober-living facility in California, though the shadow of his past looms ever close.

Frank, who is in his late twenties and is the father of two young children, lives with his wife, Betty, in a docile suburb in earshot of a Michigan expressway. He smoked a dab of marijuana outside when we spoke.

"I feel like I've done so many bad things that it's bound to come back around," Frank said. Some mornings he finds it difficult to get himself out of bed, weighed down by the depression and anxiety that went untreated during the years he spent away. We had met each other at the wilderness program in New York and had connected again later at a residential facility in Massachusetts, though this was the first time we had seen each other in ten years. I told Frank I felt that he was using his past as a way to justify the poor nature of his current situation: a job he hated, two children he could not support, a marriage on the rocks and in which he hardly participated.

"You know, I never thought about it that way," he said to me.

It was exactly what he used to say in therapy. I almost wanted to believe him. Having moved inside by then, I sat in his living room strewn with children's toys, dirty clothes, dishes veiled in mildew and mold. He later told me about a situation that drew police and Child Protective Services to his house. Frank had associated with a former client from his residential program who brought drugs and a dealer to his house. The dealer blackmailed him with a photo of Frank snorting cocaine while his child slept nearby.

But that was a strange situation, he said, not the usual. I remarked that it sounded like he had put himself in that situation, though, and again he said something that felt disingenuous: He realized he screwed up and would not again. It seemed to me that he wanted to do better, to become a man and a father, but had no frame of reference. And when he had tried to reconnect with an old friend from that program, to get closure on his past, they could only relate in the way they related back then, through drugs and angst.

Jillian, who is in her late twenties and lives in Chicago, said that being a "troubled teen" was never something she had considered about herself until it was a label. "If you're sent away to a program, then you label yourself in your head that, okay, I'm a troubled teen, and it's kind of a self-fulfilling prophecy," she said. She told me about a drug arrest that befell her while in college. She recovered, she said, and was on a hopeful path toward success as a physical trainer. After seeing her brother gunned down in a drug deal gone wrong, she told me she had vowed to change. Only later did she tell me that she had been lying. She was still dealing drugs on the side and sent me a picture of Ziploc bags of marijuana.

For those who went through months and years of treatment as teenagers, there is little more they think can bring them relief if nothing worked before. Why try again when your label persists?

After reading online about all those who were dying, a survivor named Edward posted photos of a yacht and his home on the Facebook group. He offered to put anyone up who needed a place to stay and likewise said he could help with drug treatment, a type that was illegal in the United States. When I went to visit him in Guadalajara, he did not return my calls or text messages, even as I stood outside the address he had given me. A woman walking her dog told me that she had seen people come in and out of that house. I told her I believed it was a drug clinic. She said she was not so sure. As I sat in the airport terminal for my return flight, Edward called to say he was sorry. His daughter had lost his phone. I told him it was no problem, and then he asked me for money. He said he had a bad debt that needed clearing. He said his life was in danger because he had associated, again, he admitted, with the wrong people.

Through speaking with former clients, I understood that many of us had become inured to our experiences at these programs, as trauma victims often are. A typical successful graduate looks like me: someone who chanced into adulthood not because of the programs but after a later and even more traumatic period, and who is still struggling today. Every so often I was arrested, never settling into my life until recently. Even now, I am still cautious. It feels like anything might send me back.

These stories and others are available online through reputable news outlets and trusted sources, and yet the industry surrounding teen rehabilitation still thrives. The programs were and continue to be part of an unrecognized and ineffective accreditation network. The accreditation amounts to a membership, where programs can opt in to an overseeing body, like paying for false accreditation. The same scheme tricked parents into believing their children would receive an accredited education, like that at Ivy Ridge.

"Unfortunately, folks that endorse these programs don't see a problem with it when compared with the perceived risks associated with general noncompliance and intractability," said Lynne Rachlis, a child advocate in Massachusetts who recommends against wilderness and many residential programs to clinicians. "There are obviously countless professionals who regard these programs as important components of the clinical safety net for kids presenting with behavioral difficulties; otherwise how would they manage to stay in business?"

The decade that followed the Government Accountability Office inquiry has seen no increase in federal or state oversight. The programs remain unregulated and unproven. And while the 2007 GAO investigation shed light on the hiring of unqualified therapeutic staff members at these programs and cases of child neglect and abuse, Congress never pursued a future inquiry. When I spoke with representatives at the GAO in late 2017, they told me they had destroyed their files every few years and had kept nothing beyond their final reports. But those investigations focused on what happened on campus, not what happened after.

The current director of NATSAP, Megan Stokes, told me its accreditation and approval process had changed since the GAO report in 2007. "We're not an accrediting body," Stokes said. "We're a voluntary membership organization. We're most known for our conferences."

In 2008, following the government investigation, NATSAP was tasked with explaining how the organization, long seen as an accrediting body, held its members accountable. Members within the association who strayed from compliance were never corrected. An evaluation process had not been outlined for members, allowing most any program to list itself as a member. NATSAP now requires all prospective and renewal applicants to provide copies of their state licenses, state accrediting organization, and clinician licenses. "It wasn't until the congressional testimony when we decided we really need a best practices committee," Stokes said. Their board minutes are not available to the public. Complaints lodged against programs are only made available to parents or former clients. But Stokes cautioned that they should still not be considered the definitive defender of these programs. Yet, between 2017 and 2019, more than forty-seven new programs have received loose accreditation from NATSAP, bringing the total number of programs to more than 190. As of this writing, it is the only body that still oversees these programs.

Ever more frequent is the transfer of regulation by the states in which these programs operate. A state agency in Montana, which regulated these programs statewide, recently announced it was insufficiently experienced to continue overseeing the programs. The board, which oversaw sixteen for-profit programs for decades and fifty-eight complaints with no sanctions or reprimands issued, sat within the state's Department of Labor and Industry. A bill sent around the Montana senate moved licensing and oversight to the Department of Public Health and Human Services in mid-2019. Its first action against a troubled-teen program came less than a month later.

Still, problems are rampant more today than they were in years past: in January 2019, a residential treatment center for teenage girls in Utah and its clinical director were sued for abuse of a minor; in February of that year, a twenty-nine-year-old teacher from Northwest Academy in Idaho (which closed in September of the year prior, due to "low enrollment") was arrested on assault charges and for child abuse, neglect, and endangerment. These developments have emboldened some former clients to press charges, but states have found it difficult to prosecute cases of emotional abuse. The Massachusetts state police were investigating Swift River for possible crimes of abuse, but with no evidence of physical harm, the case was not brought forward.

This leaves former clients still more conflicted. Was their experience actually bad, or did they just perceive pain that was never really there? Had time warped their recollection? Or were they actually abused and taught not to report it? In one such Facebook post, an advocate for the closure of these programs and the moderator behind many survivor forums, and himself a survivor, posted:

Overall, I do believe that the Program has helped change my life and has been a major influence in the way I think and act today. Most of the time, if I really think about it, I am still apart [sic] of Cross Creek. I remember therapists, facilitators, and the staff always telling me that the program was my life. That didn't really click until life became the program. Every day, I see teenagers on the street downtown by where I work, and I know that could have been me, if my parents hadn't sent me to Cross Creek. I constantly find myself talking about the program to my mom or my fiancé, reading the Source, or calling St. George just to see what is happening. Every time the program comes up, in one way or another, a lesson for me is learned all over again. Something I will always treasure no matter where I am or what I am doing.

He simultaneously defended those who are adamant their experiences were rotten all the way through, like a woman who lived in the District of Columbia but attended Discovery Ranch in Utah more than a decade ago, a program that still operates today and was the subject of at least two inquiries helmed by NATSAP. The Department of Human Services (DHS) in Utah also investigated the program in a private inquiry never made public. "I need to do an investigation which mean [sic] I have to read through everyone's emails and determine which concerns are ones that violate our rules, statute and/or law," an investigator with the DHS in Utah told one of the clients. The client had written to complain that, during her time at Discovery Ranch, she was forced to rethink her love of women, that she was forced into practicing a religion not her own, and that she was touched and harassed by staff and faculty there. "All of these things take time and precision," the investigator continued. "You are welcome to pursue any avenue you would like, but as I have stated before, we take all concerns seriously and will investigate them."

Hearing a person in power say they can help, that they are listening, is consoling. Clients, fuming years later over injustices they experienced or saw, find a glimmer of hope in such reassurances. They are, for the first time in many years, being heard as adults and not as troubled teens. They feel empowered and hope to save others from what experiences they suffered in their earlier days. Then the clients' emails go unanswered. Their phone calls go straight to voice mail. No charges are ever brought, and they again feel lost, unheard, and cast away and forgotten anew, like that night on which they were first taken.

Hazel, Avery, Mike, and Mark returned home from their experiences to find they were ill prepared for reintegrating into society. Their friends had moved on. Their families were tougher than before. They had many restrictions and no personal space. Against loneliness, trauma, and isolation, each tried in their own way to carve for themselves a life worth living. But it proved much more difficult than any of them imagined.

2

HAZEL

Following her initial stint at the wilderness program, and after wending through more therapeutic programs and stints in residential treatment centers and therapeutic boarding schools, Hazel would find herself returning to ALE of her own volition.

Roughly ten years after she left, she packed up her car in Brooklyn, with a friend she had met while at another program, to take a job as an instructor. She had heard from Eddy that ALE was hiring. It felt like she had never left. The programs she had attended in the years since ALE, all for the treatment of her personality, which was still such an affront to her grandparents, stayed with her. Of all the schools and programs, it was her time in the wilderness that truly impressed upon her the notion that she was somehow sick, and always would be. The notion that trauma was something not best shed but embraced.

Hazel was excited for her first day back in the wilderness. She loved the outdoors, though she and her friend were ashamed to admit that it might be a love derived from the programs. "I want to show kids that you can make it out of this alive," she said. But that past, long buried and untended, revealed itself as uglier and less innocuous than Hazel had remembered. Hazel saw Donna, her former instructor, who was leading the training. It was the first time they had seen each other in roughly a decade.

"Donna, hi!" Hazel said that first day.

"Hi, Hazel," Donna said and continued walking past her like she was a ghost. Hazel felt alone and wondered again why she had come, feeling that she had made a mistake.

"Everything was the same. I remember everything, Elephant's Graveyard, campsites . . . and I just slowly was back there. I was this trapped kid," Hazel said.

Donna talked to the group of instructors about the types of clients they might encounter. "I have this one kid who thinks he's an elephant, can you believe that?" Donna said, as though the instructors should treat him like an idiot.

From there, a world was revealed to Hazel that she always knew existed but could never prove: that the instructors were not properly trained nor equipped in childcare, let alone empathized or understood child psychology. She had not taken so much as a test and had never needed to qualify for the position in any way. Everything had been a lie. Even the family bonds Hazel once believed had existed between herself and the staff had defaulted. "I remember looking at Donna and thinking, *You bitch, how dare you? Were you making fun of me to a group of fucking hippies?*"

After the training session, Hazel went into the woods by herself. She set up her tarp the same way she had been taught a decade before. As day turned to night, she set about doing all the things she had done back then, like second nature. She collected and snapped long sticks and tree limbs, sparked a fire, and watched the sun saddle the horizon, chasing the night clouds at the close of day. Stars outside breached the dusk. Around her, a vision of the future: slow, modest, resolute, and enduring. The flames grew high, then the fire's light faded to embers.

Wood cracked and turned to coal. She wondered whether she'd ever be privileged to appreciate such a place of beauty again, beauty without hate and dismay and the ruins of her childhood.

She hated feeling that she was cursed because of who she once was. She was determined, through this gesture of paying her experiences forward, to overcome that faulty person of her youth. She did not want to live up to an old idea of herself and had worked hard to get to some place where she felt she might transform her life's tribulations into something hopeful for another child. A silly thought, since this space was hers forever, so long as she maintained it.

The moon lifted higher. She brought out her dinner of rice and lentils and she cried. The plastic spork trembled as it had trembled a decade before.

The day's events did not feel like training to Hazel. "We did Turtle Phase, we weren't allowed to talk, it was all the same shit," she said. "I just broke down at one point. They put us through an actual experiential training, like a solo, so you know what the program's like for the kids."

Hazel quickly lapsed back into the fear and self-doubt and worry that her family would again abandon her. She felt alone and scared, as she had those many years before. "I just didn't move for, like, a second. It was Friday night, and I just remember feeling so fucking sad. I was just there, and I was, like, what am I doing here? They were, like, 'Hazel, you can leave at any time.'"

And she did, but only because she didn't get the job.

Like a soured relationship, it was a bitter ending to an already bitter relationship, one she had hoped to replace with something better. She now remembers the program twice with spite and rage.

She went back home to New York and rented her first real apartment with her boyfriend, in the Bushwick neighborhood. He would become her husband.

"I think I just needed to struggle," she said.

When I last spoke to her, in April 2019, she was considering a return to school for nursing or some such degree and hoping to become a singer or dancer with a local musician. Elsewhere, in New Jersey, her mother, Paula, had killed herself, completing a decades-long promise.

3

Avery

After Avery left her godmother's place, she moved into a "teen-age trap house." The residents were all friends, seventeen and eighteen years old. Though they didn't do drugs, they were rowdy. They blasted music until the cops came knocking. One night someone pulled out a pistol and shot a hole through the living room floor, a time Avery recalled as "interesting."

She maintained her job at the day care and picked up shifts working the counter at a local McDonald's. In the months to come, she met a boy through MySpace, and two weeks later they moved into an apartment together. Two months after that, Avery was pregnant. She had her first child when she was twenty-one.

When her son was eight months old, Avery came home from work to find the boy's father, her boyfriend, strung out on Vicodin, a drink in his hand. "He became a different person when he mixed them," Avery said. He fractured her eye socket and dislocated her jaw that night.

She got custody of her son and moved out. The boy's father paid one month of child support and then disappeared. Avery resorted to strip dancing at night to pay her bills, which could not be met by the day care gig alone. She broke down and called her godmother. "Can you take him for six months? I need to get my life together," Avery said, the earnestness sounding a lot like a manipulative child. "I need your help. I can't do it on my own."

The latitude granted her came at a price. Over the next decade, Avery would have two more children with two different men, shuttling between work as a bartender and living in homeless shelters. "I was with a guy that I shouldn't have been with. I ended up homeless, and I was bartending, pregnant, living in a homeless shelter, taking care of his daughter," she told me. She does not speak of a fourth, a son, whom she gave up for adoption. She then moved in with her boyfriend in Slidell. She sometimes worked as a distributor of Plexus Worldwide products, a multilevel marketing company.

When I visited Avery, I noticed that the doorjamb leading into her Slidell apartment had been splintered. At the time, she told me that someone had tried to break into the apartment when the last tenants lived there. Later, she revealed that the doorjamb had in fact been broken by her new boyfriend, who kicked it in when he became mad at her for locking him outside. Of him, she said, "I struggled so bad with depression and living my trauma and putting myself in situations that were not good for me in the end"; I did not want to point out that it seemed she had not escaped those situations.

Before I arrived, she told a neighbor, "I have this reporter coming over, so if you hear me yell, just keep your window open." She said she worries about little things, has developed an obsessive-compulsive disorder, and is now a germaphobe. I asked if she was on any medication. "I am not on any medication anymore," she told me. "I was on Celexa, and then I stopped taking medication to go the natural route," which did not seem to be working. Avery confided in me that she had spent the night prior in the emergency room after having a breakdown. She had woken up the night before and refused to touch or feed her daughter, struggling as she did with postpartum depression. She went to the emergency room to ask for a "low-dose SSRI" (selective serotonin reuptake inhibitor), just until she could see her doctor. They admitted her to a clinic, into which she willingly signed herself. "I had been diagnosed with post-traumatic stress disorder a long time ago. I have still shown the symptoms, so that diagnosis is still with me. They also diagnosed me with a borderline personality disorder. I don't know exactly what that means," she told me. "I meant to google that today."

Avery was engaged to her new boyfriend when we spoke, but she did not end up seeing the marriage through. She moved into her soon-to-be father-in-law's home nearby, after leaving her apartment in Slidell, hoping to save money and revive an old love.

Avery started sending me photos of her children and updates on her family. We exchanged text messages and phone calls, Facebook messages and emails. After meeting Avery several times, I called Greg to check in with him. I thought Greg might make a good addition to her new life plans, and I was pleased to hear that they had started to rekindle the flame from the program. Avery was even planning to make a trip out to Boston to see Greg.

"I'm excited," Greg said in a message to me shortly before the trip.

Six days before her flight, however, Avery backed out. Neither Greg nor myself, despite multiple attempts, ever heard from her again.

4

MIKE

When Mike was released from prison in 2013, he could not keep clean. The habits he had formed were too ingrained. Mike was erratic and difficult to control. He listened to nobody. He wanted to move out from under his parents' roof and watchful eye, which would eventually lead him down a path of self-destruction.

Mike had reconnected with his friend Dempsey, who was living in South Trenton. Steve, who had been released after finishing fourteen months of his sentence in Virginia on the bribery charges, drove Mike to South Trenton. It was a neighborhood more befitting a life of crime than a road to recovery. Old brick industrial buildings with broken windows were shrouded in spray paint. Trash collected in the gutters along the roadways. Seedy men in hooded sweatshirts paced at street corners.

"This is where you want to live now?" Steve said, turning to his son.

"Yeah, right here," Mike said, pointing to a derelict building.

"Good luck to you," Steve said and drove away.

Dempsey lived in a house near the stadium, off Lamberton Street. He was known around the neighborhood as the seventh white guy to ever join the Bloods in Trenton, and Mike was hoping to become the eighth. Mike instead found his calling among the Ñetas, a Puerto Rican gang. The two lived in the house on Lamberton as part of a neutral territory between both gangs. Inside, Mike rented his room to transients who worked for him, for hourly companions, while in the living room he smoked crack cocaine and sold drugs to whomever came through. They ran dogfights in the basement.

"Everybody was happy with what we were doing," Mike said of the area's gangs.

The only way out of the house around back was to scale a large brick wall. "We could block you in, stick you up, and rob your car," Mike said. "We do what we want to you, and only our little community on our block will know that you existed." If people walked in through the back door, they were locals and were charged less for the drugs. If people drove up to the house, that meant they were from the suburbs and were charged higher prices. If someone entered through one door, they were instructed to exit through a different door to ward off police suspicion. It was an "amazing amount of money, endless."

So, too, was their own addiction. They disobeyed the cardinal rule: Don't get high on your own supply. In quieter moments, they dreamed of sobriety. He and Dempsey tried a regional inpatient program to treat their addictions. Within a day, they met each other back at the house, dope sick and getting better with each new hit.

"Everything about our life was dark and negative and troublesome and problematic. I was super high on life for the first nine months after I got out of Cross Creek, and I never really thought about it again. I just moved forward," Mike said years later. "I started causing so many problems in my own life that Cross Creek became irrelevant."

Six months after his and Dempsey's first iteration of detox and rehab, Mike called his parents, who drove him from South Trenton to a Mercer County hospital for its inpatient program. With him, he brought a bag of dope. After his intake, he excused himself to a bathroom, closed the stall door behind him, and lowered the baby-changing-station table.

He scraped the inside of the wax bag, shaking out all the last bits, desperate to go down high before he committed to sobriety.

The door to the restroom opened. Through the crack in his stall, he saw two men in gray button-down shirts, like a security detail. As they pushed the door inward, they threw his body to the ground and wrapped him in what felt like a hot blanket, about the same as he remembered when he was attacked at Ivy Ridge, his life stuck on repeat.

They stripped him of his clothes and wrestled Mike into a hospital gown, his rear exposed as they shoved him into an individual room without engaging the door's magnetic lock. After they left him, Mike ran out of the room and charged down the hallway. He ran straight into another magnetically locked door, this one shut. Mike kicked the door and busted the magnet, freeing himself of his gown and bounding into the parking lot, chased by the two security guards and a phalanx of nurses. Now naked in the parking lot, Mike collided with a young girl and shouted, "She grabbed my dick!"

"Crazy on drugs, right? Butt naked. Yelling at this girl for sexually harassing me by grabbing my dick, now nobody wants to touch me," Mike said years later. The hospital did not readmit him.

He and Dempsey went back to running the trap house, paranoid once more, worried that people were coming for them at all hours, a deep psychosis at the bottom of the deepest void of addiction. Then one day, while Mike was holding down the operations in South Trenton, Dempsey was alone at his mother's home. Standing in the kitchen, he tied himself off and drove a needle into an available, pleading vein. His baby's mother was not at home, nor was his child, and so he had a moment to himself. The satisfaction came and left at once, leaving him to collapse on the kitchen floor, convulsing in the shriveled grip of an overdose, where his mother would come to find him later. At the hospital, Dempsey lay in a coma, and his mother, Nancy, called Mike.

"You should come say your goodbyes to CK," she told Mike. "He is going to die."

"I said goodbye to him," Mike said years later. It was not a catalyst to getting sober.

Displeasure and strain are what led him to Carrier Clinic, a white brick building advertised on commuter rails and billboards across the state. Mike would revisit the clinic many times. It would be years before he took the treatment seriously, following a referral to Delray Beach, Florida, and many more months of working twelve-step programs, between which he continued pimping out women from rehab facilities in Delray Beach and selling guns and drugs on the side. As he sobered up for ever-longer stretches of time, putting a wicked past and a terrible temptation behind him, his first real day of sobriety came on December 11, 2015. Mike began to reminisce about his time in the various programs, his transgressions, and watched the high recede for the final time, as he realized his consequences. He remembered everything in his sober clarity. He would soon be twenty-five years old. Practically a man. Miraculously he had survived this long, and his outlook toward life changed. He had tired of the home invasions, of stealing cars. He had tired of himself.

While working the twelve steps of Narcotics Anonymous, Mike called everyone he had harmed—for the robbery for which he says he served more than three years in prison, for the drug-possession charges he racked up in Florida, for the year he did in county lockup that led him to meet Dempsey—and ticked down his list of "everybody I hurt and robbed or whatever." He still felt there was blame left to place on the Lieutenant and Jason Finlinson at Ivy Ridge.

"I had, you know, the occasional flashback of emotions, for something would make me think of Ivy Ridge, let's say, and I would remember this feeling flare up in me . . . if I could go back today and do it again, I would . . . I want them to feel how I feel," he said years later of Finlinson and the others. "But Ivy Ridge really hurt me, really bad, honestly.

"I have been through a lot and all, but I do remember it was really messed up, man. I was just a child. I was only a child."

———

Mike came to have his revenge on Finlinson, though far from a cinematic end.

I called Mike on Valentine's Day in 2018 and told him I was interested in learning more about what happened to him after he left his last program. After we spoke, he started watching a show on Netflix "about these girls that are locked up in a juvenile prison, but not exactly."

"I start watching it," Mike told me, "and I am listening to the girls do their interviews on camera and I am watching the staff do their version of what the girls are talking about. Seems familiar. I knew immediately they are in one of these programs, because those are the same things we used to say as kids and that's the same thing the staff would tell our parents to smooth over the truth. I remember this clear feeling sad. I felt so sad. I know what that girl is trying to tell us and the viewers, that don't know that these programs exist, have no idea what is happening."

He had similarly experienced lonesomeness and had tried to voice it himself but went unheard. This was something new for him, this empathy by proxy. He had never liked watching cop shows or investigation series about criminals. "There is no entertainment, for me, to watch people get locked up," he said.

He started searching online for more information about the places from his past, and eventually he entered the network of survivor groups. What he found was "whack, totally ignorant, just small-minded—like feminists and vegans. That's how I look at people calling themselves program survivors. Super whack and lame, bro." He held himself and Mark (even me, for my own stunts) accountable for their own actions and believed his parents were not to blame, nor were the programs, for anything suffered later. "There is no way I can believe that every place was as bad as all of the kids are saying. Even the kids that are grown, that are our age now. Some of them are much older. I think a lot of them are weak, soft people that are not accountable and don't want to grow up and just face reality," he told me. "This was the truth: I was an out-of-control kid. You were out of control. My brother was out of control. My parents tried everything to get us under control, make us better. They had no other options. This is what they thought was the best. They didn't do it to hurt me or Mark."

But the web has an allure. Enough time spent staring at videos or in chat rooms can change someone's opinion. Mike found himself caught up in the stories and comment sections of the online survivor forums. He found websites decrying the programs he was in and realized that, while he was building a life, others had been seeking revenge. While he was working to put those years behind him, others were struggling toward retribution. He had never heard of the allegations or complaints levied against his programs, had no clue there were people rallying against them. He came across videos of the fights and beatdowns at Ivy Ridge.

"I was in these videos, standing there," he said.

He rewatched the beatdowns he had witnessed firsthand. He watched one video in which a man returns to the now-abandoned Ivy Ridge campus and explores the rooms where Mike was held. The videos triggered mixed emotions and memories of all his interactions with staff. Finlinson. Mike remembered him in particular.

"Now I am engulfed in reliving these realities," he told me.

Mike posted his contact information, hoping to hear back from kids he knew at Ivy Ridge. He trudged through the comment section and found a woman who seemed to post across many different forum pages. He did not know who the woman was or why she wanted to know about which programs he went to or if he had any dealings with Finlinson. It turned out she was Finlinson's ex-wife.

The woman offered to fly Mike to Las Vegas, to testify against her former husband in a child-custody case. "I told her these are my terms: if I go, there is no guarantee I show up," he said. In the intervening years, Mike told me, he had become a professional gambler and was looking for an excuse to go back to Vegas. "I told her, 'I don't know you, I don't know him as a father,'" Mike said. "'I might just literally rob you for a flight.'"

When I told Mike that I wanted to join him in the courthouse in St. George, Utah, he began ignoring my calls and text messages. After several days, he sent me a message:

> I came to Vegas. I'm going to St. George this morning. Sorry for the late response. I was in deep contemplation over this. I have moved on, nonetheless he damaged me in powerful ways. I appreciate what happened, but resent the way it did. I'm not sure I'll say anything, but maybe just to see him will remind me I have moved on a long time ago. Or maybe it will refresh memories of my life then. I'm unsure. It's a sensitive journey, risking opening the wound. Either way, in no way is his relationship with her my place, and I've certainly grown to be an adult and live a positive life in business and spirituality. I'm a man of God and fulfilled with growth and happiness.

Mike arrived at the courthouse late, forgetting that there was a time-zone change between Nevada and Utah. In the courtroom, Mike saw Finlinson, his lawyer, his new wife, and the woman with whom he had been speaking on the phone. He took a hard look at Finlinson and sat down. "Turns out he is a freaking loser," Mike said. "Who knew?"

The woman took the stand and had trouble speaking, under fire from the defense attorneys and the judge. Mike sat and watched, feeling sorry for the stranger, unsure of whether her inability to speak and defend herself was a result of the accident that disabled her or something more. After questioning, the judge asked the woman whether she had any character witnesses to prove what she claimed about her ex-husband: that he had a history of mistreating children. Mike was the only one in the room, his face a scrawl of tattoo ink. The judge said the court would recess, which the gavel reiterated.

During the break, according to Mike, Finlinson approached Mike and extended his hand.

"Do I know you?"

"Maybe," Mike responded.

"Okay," Finlinson said and walked away. Mike recalled the interaction as "almost with this *This is how we are going to play it?* attitude."

Mike met the woman in person for the first time.

"Hello," she said. "Can you help carry me? There's a place next door. I can buy you lunch."

They stumbled together the half block from the courthouse to the restaurant, her hand slung into the crook of Mike's arm. He was feeling less willing to speak to the judge but by then had become so curious about the other side of Finlinson that he ate with her and asked about her family. But she seemed agitated. He asked about her father, her siblings, her children. "Every time I did that she acted as if she couldn't hear me," Mike said a year later. "She checked her phone, waited thirty seconds, and went back to whatever she was saying." He thought she was a "wretched" woman.

Back inside the courtroom, Mike approached the bench and was sworn in by the judge. He took a seat at the stand and looked out over the dismal courtroom, filled with empty seats and the man he credited with much of the abuse he endured throughout his time at Ivy Ridge. It felt for a moment that he was on the stand speaking for everyone from those programs.

Since the woman had no attorney, she cross-examined Mike.

"Did you see Jason Finlinson hit anybody with a Maglite?"

"No, I have never seen him do that."

"Have you ever seen Jason . . . ?"

The questions carried on like a volley, served between the two with no real progress.

"The truth is," Mike said a year later, "if she was smarter, which she wasn't, she would ask me more in-depth questions."

Mike was cross-examined by Finlinson's attorney. Afterward, Mike turned to the judge and said, "I can just tell you that Jason Finlinson beats kids. I have never seen him beat his own kids. I didn't even know he had kids."

According to Mike, the judge looked down across the room at Finlinson's former wife and said, "I grew up on a farm and that's considered discipline. It's not abuse, it's just discipline."

————

Mike returned to Florida, where he continued as an active member in twelve-step programs. When I went to meet him for follow-up interviews, he was hard to reach. We came to meet at a café late one night in December 2018. We had tea and club soda and he rehashed some details that had troubled me. Behind him, his Audi A7 was parked in the parking lot. At one point, he called me a "depressed gay" for being a writer, which felt more like he was dealing with his own insecurities about his face full of tattoos.

The children admitted to these programs learned at a young age to manipulate much more deftly in environments of great restraint. After years of navigating the whims of programs and institutions, they had internalized a manipulation of their own perception. They were not the victims any longer but, rather, the restless souls of bygone children. They wanted to play games that were no longer age appropriate. Like Mike, many wanted to fit in with the general populace while still taking advantage where they could. Mike got a free trip to Las Vegas under the auspices of reconciliation, and Mark told me once about the rush he felt when a teller gave him the wrong change and he left the store twenty dollars richer.

As Mike and I sat at the café, two cars collided on Route 1, and we went to go see the accident. We had our phones out, but by the time we reached the road's edge, the police had already arrived. We walked back to our table, passing his all-white Audi. The lies kept stacking as the question of his face tattoos, which seemed to me an escalating product of his time spent within institutions. If he had been mistreated and abused, maybe there was something to the tattoos offering him a veil, something to distance him from society or to dissuade roughhousing.

"All they brought was negativity in my life," he said. "I'm a real-dealing professional, you know what I mean? I have a career. I don't even curse anymore." I gave him that. He really had stopped cursing, at least when we spoke. It was not always enough, however, because the appearance of those tattoos restricted his ability to eat at some restaurants, to stay at some hotels. They also tempted young gunrunners and gangbangers, who would think they had found a solo target.

"I'm in jeopardy of my past for sure, one million percent," he said. "These young jitz, they want to try me, man, and kids who have, like, a couple little face tattoos, they maybe didn't earn it and they are, like, 'Oh, he has got more. I need to get him.' You know what I mean? I am an easy target for that stuff."

He told me it was something that worried him. It was a lifestyle for which he was still paying, despite wanting to wash away the past and forge a better future as the past knocked often and reared its ugly head. His problems lived in his shadow, which was perhaps why he felt most comfortable in the dark, in constant struggle with the world. It is also why, he said, he kept beneath the driver seat of his car a Glock 19 with an extended clip for extra bullets.

Despite the troubled road ahead for Mike, he noted that he was proud of his brother, Mark, worried though he was for his eventual release from probation. They rarely talked, however, choosing instead to use their father as a go-between. Steve always called to check on the boys, even when I was with them.

Soon those calls from Steve were to me directly, followed by a string of emails in early 2019.

"I'm praying for Mark daily. I love him very much. Keep calling him, see if he wants to go to treatment," he wrote to me in April of that year. "His family loves him, and I hope he lets us back into his life."

5

MARK

When Mark left Sorenson's Ranch just a few weeks shy of his eighteenth birthday, freedom entered him like a shot of adrenaline. He bolted straight into the open world with no particular goal or destination.

"I'm thinking, great, life's good," he said. "No one's watching me."

He bounced between Boston, California, and Florida, hitchhiking or crashing with friends and selling weed as he went, along the way landing for a spell in Montana with Wilson, the friend he had made while at Cross Creek. With his mother's blessing, Mark moved into a house with Wilson and several of Wilson's relatives: his cousin, his cousin's girlfriend, and his brother.

Friendships formed in the programs were almost never beneficial to long-term success. Living with Wilson, Mark's entire world was composed of young adults who had fallen into the darkest maws of adolescence. Their world was small and their days of little substance: sitting around on the couch, watching television, and doing drugs. Their time in recovery was a distant memory.

Wilson's father owned a telemarketing company, and Wilson and Mark both began working there to earn some money to feed themselves and their continued drug addictions. Their only other responsibility was the care of the family dogs, three purebred and hearty pit bulls, when the father went out of town on business.

While Wilson was away on a business trip with his father, Mark asked the cousin to drive him out of state to meet a young blonde girl in Arizona, whom he had been calling and promising that he might come visit. Wilson's cousin was also looking to get away, and quickly agreed. The cousin, his girlfriend, and Mark piled into their SUV. In the back were the dogs, a collection of family jewelry, a stack of money, an ounce of pot, and a handgun.

After several hours on the road, they pulled off the interstate somewhere in the Idaho panhandle. They spent the night in a hotel and continued their drive south in the morning, careening and smoking as they traversed the interstate. When they reached Ogden, Utah, several hundred miles from Montana, they pulled off into a gas station and moseyed through an attached convenience store. When they emerged, a police cruiser had pulled into the parking lot. The cruiser followed them back onto the highway, and eventually the suspicious officers witnessed a petty infraction that gave the officers cause to pull the SUV over.

When the police searched the car, they discovered the stash and marijuana scattered throughout the center console and the floorboards. The police took Mark to a youth detention facility, where he called his parents to ask for help. They refused.

"You will be eighteen in a couple of weeks. That's it, we're done with you." He wilted for two weeks in lockup, until he found out that he would not be charged since he was a minor. Eventually, his parents caved and bought him a one-way bus ticket to return home via Newark.

"I think they were just, like, 'This is our son, we let him feel the pain, tough love, whatever,'" Mark told me.

Mark eventually returned to New Jersey. His paranoia had given rise to future addiction. Now eighteen years old, he found navigating social circles outside of programs and institutions increasingly difficult.

He misplaced his trust, believing that relationships were mutually beneficial, like at Cross Creek where Wilson became a fast friend merely by proxy. This errant trust led him one day to Asbury Park, a beach town on the Jersey shoreline. Beneath the heavy sodium lights of an outdoor park, a friend handed him a pipe.

"What is it?" Mark asked.

"It's just coke," said the friend, someone Mark had recently met and hardly knew. "Same stuff, just that you smoke it."

"That's crack, man."

"Nah, it's just coke."

Mark shrugged, grabbed the pipe, and inhaled, forming an addiction he would maintain for years. Over the next several years, the cocaine, crack, and later heroin followed him. In the haze of addiction, a blur to him and his family, he would be charged with the possession of a deadly weapon (a butter knife, he says) and drug possession, which led him into days cascading into nearly a decade spent siphoned into and out of various treatment centers and prison cells. He had become a habitual offender before the age of twenty. He "shot dope and coke every day [alone]." In no particular order, and without haste, he became everything his parents had paid to prevent.

In January 2017, Mark escaped a drug-treatment program to which he was confined after a prison stint. In the program, back in central New Jersey and somewhat close to home, he shot up more heroin. When the staff and faculty found out, he bolted, and a nationwide warrant was issued for his arrest. If caught, he would return again to the cold prison cell from which he had come. "What I know in my life is do good, do shitty, do good, do worse, do even worse, do good, do worse, do good, do really bad, do good. It gets worse every time," Mark said.

When the New Jersey state police found Mark in 2017, he was lying on the ground, propped onto a stone walkway. He was struggling to his feet. His clothes were sodden and bespattered. His jeans were ripped open at the knees, tears from which blood dribbled. His face was scratched and bruised. Inside, his kidneys were failing.

He identified himself to the police officer but had trouble with his words. He stated that he had a drug problem, that his legs were hurting because he had been sleeping outdoors for the last two days, and his back was in agony. When he was searched by the officers, they found nine wax folds of heroin, five white-topped glass vials of crack cocaine, and five hypodermic needles. Mark was charged, prosecuted, and remanded to prison after emergency surgery to save his liver.

Eventually he stabilized and withdrew from the drugs in a new cell in a new ward. He felt, as he always had, apart from the world, but with the comforts of a prisonlike home. "I never forget I went to these programs," Mark said years later, between check-in phone calls with his parole officer. "We don't live our lives based on these programs. But I remember them."

———

Mark and I hugged on the porch leading into his apartment on the first day we saw each other in more than a decade. His girlfriend and dogs were inside. I hugged them too. His girlfriend, who would cycle out of his life after I made the first of several visits over two years, did not like me. They had met at a drug-treatment program after they were in county lockup together. I told Mark that, statistically speaking, it was incredible that he was still breathing. National overdose deaths were rising, I said, and it would be a miracle if he survived another relapse. It was good that he was sober and, by all appearances, happy and doing well. His girlfriend frowned at me. Mark, on the other hand, giggled in a way that transported me back ten years to a much simpler time, when we were, as it is said, just kids. It was his laugh, his smile, through which I saw no pain but, rather, promise.

Mark was a friend before I knew I had any, one who would welcome me into his home years after parting ways and treat me as though I were an older brother. When we spoke about his incarcerations and struggle with drugs, I felt an overwhelming sense that I was speaking to myself, a version of a life I might have led but luckily escaped. Mark was out on parole, nearly finished with a court-ordered drug program. He spent his mornings driving garbage truck routes around northern New Jersey. When I visited him, his apartment was tidy and his dogs well fed.

"As soon as I got out of prison the last time, I kept a routine," Mark told me. "It's my own routine. It's the routine that I chose. I could choose any routine under the sun, and I chose this one. All these programs and incarcerations in my life, and I was never the controlling factor of my routine. Yeah, I have a plan to keep it going."

We talked about many things, among them how we found irony in our parents saying children's brains are like sponges and expecting us to forget being taken, and how we could not stop laughing when we discussed trauma or frustrating moments in our lives, like the regrets that led each of us on our own paths in and out of jail. I confessed to him with a smile that I, too, had far too many run-ins with Johnny Law. It seemed the only way to bring up the story, despite the hardships suffered. I think they call it empathy. It was not a defense mechanism, I believe, but rather a childish notion of the self. We still had not shed that solemn indifference born of youth.

Anyway, we weren't there to commiserate or throw a pity party. I asked him questions about him and his brother, Mike, and his family, who eventually invited me over for dinner to try those chicken burgers Mark had always raved about. We drove to the family farm, and I met with Mark and his father for about an hour. There was a fire in the hearth and an animal mewed outside. Mark and his father chatted while I sat.

"The bottom line is where we are today," Steve said. "Thing is, you're still young. And everybody has an opportunity to put their lives on track. So I don't think that that's a problem, in my opinion. As long as you stay off of drugs, I know your life is going to be fine. I know you'll be successful work-wise. I know you'll be successful as a person. I see that you're growing in a positive way. So even though I think you wasted a lot of years with drugs and getting in jail and all that, I think the fact of the matter is that I think you'll get your act together anyway. I think you'll be fine anyway. Like, okay, that was what it was, move on."

Mark said he felt that he had wasted much of his life. Nearly ten years. But he was conflicted. He couldn't decide whether wasting it was worthwhile, given the experiences and life lessons that had brought him to this sober state. He was also happy for the first time, with both a job and a steady girlfriend. How could a road that led him there be all that bad?

We spoke briefly about Mike and recovery, and there was a moment when I felt that perhaps they would all start racing again, which would seem a nice coda to their complicated story.

Then, after an hour, once Steve had left the room, Mark leaned in and said, "For years I hated him, I didn't want anything to do with him. I didn't want to do anything with his business. But deep down, I was, like, that's still a man. That's still a man in my life. A couple of years ago, I don't remember what the situation was, but it just clicked. I was, like, that's my dad. I got to respect him, I got to treat him right."

After I drove back home that night, I sent a text message to Mark. "Thanks for having me over, dude," I said.

"Of course, man," he wrote back. "We appreciated having you."

Then he sent another message a few minutes later, to tell me his father had randomly texted him for the first time ever to tell him that he loved him. To tell him he was a good kid.

After our meeting, a question kept nagging me: What does it mean to be good despite a terrible past? Mark's life had come around, returning to the point of its doomed departure and from where he might set off again, to anywhere he may dream. But, instead, he chose something more nightmarish.

On supervised release, Mark was a rock star. He went to work each day and lived with his girlfriend in a modest apartment in a housing development not far from the garbage truck depot where, at 3:00 a.m. each morning, he would report for work clean shaven and sober. His eyes were often bright, no longer hazy and gray the way I had always known him. But he told me how worried he was about the end of his parole nearing. He feared that knowing no one was watching would be an easy way for him to foul up.

Then the supervised release program ended, and with it so too went he. In no particular order, Mark:

- started drinking;
- may have started smoking crack, because he became paranoid that people were watching him;
- told me his dad put a tracking device on his car, to follow his movements, and that was why he was in Newark, not to get drugs like he did in the past but to see if his father would call, worried that his son had relapsed;
- yelled at his father when he called;
- issued restraining orders against his mother, father, and Mike;
- was left by his girlfriend and her daughter, who severed all communication;
- told me he thought I was part of a bigger conspiracy to keep him down and under control; I asked him what control he meant, but he did not know.

For Hanukkah, I had given Mark a paintball jersey (one grandfathered to me by an old friend, a jersey I kept as a keepsake of a time I remembered fondly, before everything fell apart), a gesture I hoped he would pay forward. He had started playing the sport again, and for the holiday, I had brought him a bag of all my old gear and attire, including the jersey with my name on it. I hoped it would be a reminder that I had suffered and lived and, in some way, hoped that he would know he could live too. Now, since his falloff, it was just a jersey. For the first time the tables had turned. I felt the anguish of my parents. I did not know what to do.

I wanted to help, and that desire counted for nothing.

Steve agreed and then, as this book was being fact-checked, undergoing a legal review and final copyedit, wished to not participate. Without fail, he had watched his sons slip in and out of harm's way, the brothers listing always toward damnation. I thought that hearing about Steve's situation might help others. I was met only by defeat.

"Incidentally I can not offer hope to anyone," he said in our final email exchange, "the situation is absolutely hopeless."

EPILOGUE

L ooking backward hurts. It is a constant struggle. I struggle with my past the way I struggle with my present. I struggle today knowing that some of my wrongs cannot be undone. I struggle knowing that bad memories of bad people and worse places and actions will revisit me as though they happened yesterday, that the distance I put from feelings and people amounts to nothing more than time, never redemption. Though uncomfortable, it is necessary to wade through the bogs of my past in order to more soundly preserve a better future. In this struggle, I find opportunities to try again.

I chanced into adulthood.

The administrators at the various facilities I attended cautioned against clients returning home too early. Clients were often seen as unfit to return to society before finishing the programs, so recommendations for either an upgrade or a gradual step-down to less-intensive treatment were far more common than simple release. Instead of returning to a high school or community college environment (many clients were barred from returning to high school), some clients were shipped off to boarding schools that lacked the therapeutic component. Others were sent to outpatient substance abuse facilities near their home. Others still were sent on to stricter, more therapeutic-intensive programs, which seemed redundant to the clients: How much worse could it get? Many simply pleaded for juvenile detention, where at least they would be close to home, able to communicate with their friends through handwritten letters.

Removing a client for long periods from the environment into which they will return can damage an already frail psyche. It disrupts their discourse and the way they relate to friends and family. It distances them more from the world they're meant to join. They come home with something to prove, time for which they must account.

Many child advocates and psychologists believe that a decent and successful compromise is sending a child to wilderness therapy, letting them experience the outdoors while they sober up, rooting them in the moment rather than the chaos of their school days, before being sent home. A few weeks can be shrugged off as a minor derailment. It does not devastate a child's sense of community, fellowship, and dignity.

But questions remain for me. How many of these kids would have died if they hadn't been exposed to any form of "treatment"? Was their fate inevitable, given the path they were on, or would they have simply "grown out of" their destructive behavior?

What has frustrated me over the years I spent reporting for and writing this book was how often I heard lies. Blatant, unfounded, hysterical lies.

In numerous phone calls, text messages, emails, and in-person interviews, the subjects of this book and those who corroborated stories about the programs told me they were happy and living fulfilling lives. They would say how deeply they wished this project and the stories born of it—for magazines or newspapers—would help others struggling the way they had struggled. Then, after several hours (and often when the audio recorder was turned off), they would reveal that life was not so good, that they had a recent encounter with law enforcement or a psych ward or generalized destitution. One person could not comprehend why his parents were threatening to cut him off financially. He was twenty-seven.

Many would ask me for money. They would ask for royalties from this book. They would ask to speak with my editors, demanding a payday or editorial oversight. They would threaten me professionally and personally, exhibiting many of the similar emotional spasms and insecurities that, I imagined, had gotten them sent away in the first place. They would seek in many ways to question my own intentions, believing that I would defend the programs and sully their names. In their threats, they were vindictive, a misplaced anger I attributed to the social leeriness born of these programs. Each time, in whatever mode of communication, I witnessed the reversal of their intentions and the vanishing of their stories, which then seemed more like a cover. But I couldn't blame them. I didn't think that, after years of forced adjustment, they could be faulted for blaming everyone but themselves.

For years I believed that I had made it out unscathed. I scorned anyone who complained about the programs, called them feckless. They wrote in online survivor groups about how their lives were ruined by the abuse—physical, sexual, emotional, imagined—that they had suffered. They pointed to experiences that seemed alien to me. I avoided them when I could.

Seeing the parade of those who died after leaving the programs made all those complaints that I'd brushed off suddenly unavoidable, made me realize I, too, wasn't so far from their fate.

My memory of the decade after I left my last program is hazy. Names and places aren't easily recalled, and some recollections that feel like my own are only lies, stories I've told dozens of times until they became indistinguishable from real memories. I told everyone I was happy, but I was miserable. I said I had a good relationship with my parents but rarely spoke to them, except when I needed cash. I said I was just an introvert, but my peers all felt like strangers. I spent time in juvenile detention for attempted armed robbery and then county jail for increasingly worse and more-serious offenses. I bought a handgun and placed the muzzle to my temple and missed.

When the parents of troubled kids ask me whether I benefited from the programs, I shy away from answering them, knowing what I know about outcomes. It's hard to say whether all those children I knew would have done even worse without the programs. There's no easy prescription. Far as I can tell, I never really shed that troubled past. I disrespect authority figures. I make risky financial decisions. I test the limits of my family's patience. My love of risk still sends me places others would prefer not to go. And I still smile when others ask about it all.

At night I remember at least two clients, once my roommates, who are now dead. There is no guilt in being alive, only shame. At the program in Utah, I struggled with sleepless nights. One of my roommates there had told me that it was better in the desert than at his last program, a lockdown somewhere in the wilds of California. He'd gone there years before, when he was fourteen, his life spent in and out of a shadowy system he still could not quite understand. He did not know how he was fitted for each program or what they were designed to change within him. What he did know was that he was now thankful to be in a program where, at night, he could not hear the screams of someone having a violent traumatic fit in the room next door.

When he and the others were asleep, I found myself one evening creeping past the sleeping guard who patrolled our rooms. I stumbled a few paces into the bathroom and brought with me a plastic bag in which I kept a black ballpoint pen, a marbled journal, and a pill. The pill was white, an *M* stamped on one side and *321* on the other, a lorazepam for the treatment of anxiety and insomnia, its origin a mystery. On the floor, in the grout between the white tiles, I crushed the pill and snorted it through the body of the pen. Then I felt for the sewing needle I kept in the spine of the journal. I dipped the sharpened point into the pen ink and drove the needle into my abdomen. Several dozen times, I carved digits like a cattle brand into my flesh.

Self-mutilation takes many forms and always springs from doubt. There is the doubt that things had always been terrible or that things are irreparable. There is the doubt that the harm will offer relief and that there is some less painful healer. At seventeen years old, pain had become a comrade.

When I had found the pill earlier that day, I was between therapy sessions. In the morning, I had shoveled horse shit in below-freezing weather in gloves that chapped the skin. Then I had spent part of the day rehashing my childhood with a therapist, to establish all the ways I had wronged everyone in my life. At the therapist's urging, I pledged to never drink or smoke or do drugs again so long as I lived.

This program would be my last in a string of camps and schools all striving to "fix me," but in many ways I never left. Now as a sober adult with a family of my own, I realize I have carried that winter with me ever since. I gave myself that scar, a jailhouse tattoo, while on the bathroom floor. The numbers are still etched into my skin today: 601. It is a police code for a child delinquent. I felt then that, if I was to be branded, I wanted to be in control of when and where and how I was marked. When I touch the scar today, I think back to the dead and often wonder whether they won out in the end.

I have never been a good sleeper, but my insomnia seems to have gotten worse over time. Ever since the night I was taken, errant sounds send me bolting upright. Footsteps in a hallway, the slamming of a car door, an unidentifiable pitter-patter. Sometimes I wake in a sweat, certain they are standing at the foot of my bed again. At night I make the rounds and check the window locks and the dead bolt on the bedroom door.

Then I check them again.

RESOURCES

It is an undertaking shouldered with the best of intentions and carried out in the most novice of atmospheres. Parenting is a crucible of learning and relearning. We relive our greatest of joys, our darkest of fears. There is no handbook for parenting, my mother always said, and life will present us lessons until we successfully master them—throughout all of life, not only in adulthood, but especially in adolescence.

Many books helped me in my search to better understand the private programs and systems in place for wayward teens. Among them were Maia Szalavitz's *Help at Any Cost* and David L. Marcus's *What It Takes to Pull Me Through*. Another insightful read into modern parenting of difficult teenagers is *The Good News About Bad Behavior*, by Katherine Reynolds Lewis. I also revisited several books that were instrumental to my own self-actualization, spirituality, and meditation while away: *The Secret*, by Rhonda Byrne; *The Four Agreements*, by Don Miguel Ruiz; the King James Bible, the Talmud, and the Torah; and *The Lion, the Witch and the Wardrobe*, by C. S. Lewis.

Below I have compiled a few federal, state, and nonprofit resources, for parents and teenagers who are looking to help pull themselves and their families through.

For Parents

Adult Children of Alcoholics

   https://www.adultchildren.org

Al-Anon/Alateen

   https://al-anon.org/newcomers/teen-corner-alateen/

Alcoholics Anonymous

   https://www.aa.org

American Academy of Child and Adolescent Psychiatry

   https://www.aacap.org

American Psychiatric Association: *Healthy Minds. Healthy Lives.*

http://apahealthyminds.blogspot.com/

Child Care Aware

https://www.childcareaware.org

Community Alliance for the Ethical Treatment of Youth

https://www.facebook.com/CAFETY/

Depression and Bipolar Support Alliance

https://www.dbsalliance.org

International Society for Traumatic Stress Studies

https://www.istss.org

Mental Health America

https://www.mhanational.org/

Nar-Anon

https://www.nar-anon.org

Narcotics Anonymous

https://www.na.org

National Alliance on Mental Illness

https://www.nami.org

National Association for the Education of Young Children

https://www.naeyc.org

National Center for Victims of Crime

https://www.victimsofcrime.org/

National Institute of Mental Health

https://www.nimh.nih.gov

National Institute on Alcohol Abuse and Alcoholism

https://www.niaaa.nih.gov

National Institute on Drug Abuse

https://www.drugabuse.gov/

National Mental Health Consumers' Self-Help Clearinghouse

https://www.mhselfhelp.org

National Resource Center on Homelessness and Mental Illness

https://www.coalitionforthehomeless.org/resources/national-resource-center-on-homelessness-and-mental-illness/

Office of National Drug Control Policy

https://www.usa.gov/federal-agencies/office-of-national-drug-control-policy

Parent/Professional Advocacy League

https://www.ppal.net

Parents. The Anti-Drug.

http://www.theanti-drug.com/

Partnership for Drug-Free Kids

https://drugfree.org/

Sidran Institute: Traumatic Stress Education & Advocacy

https://www.sidran.org

Substance Abuse and Mental Health Services Administration

https://www.samhsa.gov

The Joint Commission

https://www.jointcommission.org/

Troubled Teen Help

https://troubledteenhelp.com

FOR TEENAGERS

Children's Defense Fund

    https://www.childrensdefense.org

Florence Crittenton Home

    https://www.flocrit.org

Jane Doe Inc.

    https://www.janedoe.org

National Domestic Violence Hotline

    https://www.thehotline.org/

National Suicide Prevention Lifeline

https://www.suicidepreventionlifeline.org/

Call 1-800-273-8255

Reddit

/r/stopdrinking

/r/stopsmoking

Youth.gov

https://youth.gov/youth-topics/teen-dating-violence/resources

SELECTED SOURCES

The below compilation of sources is by no means exhaustive. More than one hundred interviews, with the help of nearly a dozen research assistants over three years, went toward furthering what academic and journalistic coverage had existed before and touched on this nationwide sector of punitive rehabilitation. What is included here is intended to shed further light toward understanding my research methodology and inquiry process. Where I have not added notes, I wish for those articles or publications to stand without comment. Where listed, to further transparency, I note attempted interviews and personal research folders by name as they appear in my research filings. In the interest of increased disclosure, I have also included details about the four main sources and how and when we discussed their stories. Notes that begin with a phrase in italics refer to those specific places in the text.

Prologue

"Jackie" first wrote to me via Twitter in June 2017, after I had published a story in the *New York Times* about my time at a residential treatment ranch in Utah. It was the first instance when I had doubts about my own approach to writing and internalizing the programs. We had later conversations through WhatsApp in November of that year and again in January 2018, as she told me more about her own struggles as the mother of a "troubled teen," conversations that ultimately led to the writing of this book.

The very first story I wrote about these programs was for Narratively: "The Night My Parents Had Me Kidnapped" (https://narratively. com/the-night-my-parents-had-me-kidnapped/), a title that bothered my parents. They felt it was a character assassination. The story explored the days and months that led to my eventual "kidnapping," a piece in which I accepted much of the responsibility for my actions and absolved my parents. My mother, to this day, has not read it.

Telep, Trisha. "The Man Who Takes Troubled Youths to Therapy Camp." *BBC News*, April 22, 2014. https://www.bbc.com/news/ magazine-26513805.

The cost of Adirondack Leadership Expeditions (ALE) was pulled from the "enrollment agreement" (http://www.heal-online.org/ adirondackcontract1.pdf), a copy of which I found through HEAL, or Human Earth Animal Liberation, which bills itself as "an artistic expression and reflection as well as a place for intellectual discourse and effective advocacy." The website plays host to accurate, in-depth documentation, news updates, staff and faculty lists, and testimonials from parents and former clients and offers a lifeline to "survivors" who wish to report abuse. In the instance of ALE, some of those abuses, not listed in this book, include using snow and ice as sanitary napkins in below-freezing temperatures; group urination and defecation, to prevent clients from running away while in private; and carving utensils out of wood and drinking excessive amounts of water, the failure to do either leading to physical punishments such as dragging a sled filled with five-gallon jugs of water up a mountain, according to client and parent testimonials.

Adolescence has always been turbulent: From *What It Takes to Pull Me Through: Why Teenagers Get in Trouble—and How Four of Them Got Out* by David L. Marcus (Boston: Houghton Mifflin, 2005). My approach to the formatting of this paragraph is similar to that in Marcus's book, which explored in detail life at the Academy at Swift River years before the students in this book arrived there, including myself. I have updated the websites and added statistics to help show the trajectory of growth these programs exhibited from then through now.

All the lives chronicled in the following pages: More than one hundred former clients were interviewed when I first set out to report this story, initially intended for newspaper and magazine articles. Through these interviews, both with clients I had known and those I had never met, I decided on the four included in this book. My decision was made after hearing all stories and then deciding on which stories reflected the four most frequently heard. These interviews were mostly conducted in person but were also conducted via Facebook Messenger, WhatsApp, and telephone calls. When interviewing educational consultants, I was fortunate enough to have the assistance of a PhD candidate, who phoned, emailed, and interviewed dozens of those consultants.

Book I: Wilderness

The letter excerpts that lead each chapter were provided by Hazel and are included in her "Source Material" folder. They are reprinted here, without edits, with the permission of Hazel's grandfather. Interviews with Hazel were conducted in person on October

17, 2017, and October 23, 24, and 25, 2018. Those interviews were supplemented by Signal phone calls and chats and Facebook Messenger exchanges over three years. The "Source Material" folder provided by Hazel and her grandfather includes dozens of documents from her time away, including psychological evaluations, letters home, and correspondence between her therapist and her grandparents. Many years on, clients have clung to such documentation in hopes of one day finding a use for it, if not because they are unsure of whether they can simply discard their past.

"complex cognitive behavior, personality expression, decision making, and moderating social behavior": University of Rochester Medical Center. "Understanding the Teen Brain." Health Encyclopedia. Accessed December 25, 2019. https://www.urmc.rochester.edu/encyclopedia/content.aspx?ContentTypeID=1&ContentID=3051.

ten to twenty thousand kids experience a furloughed youth each year: This estimate is garnered from my reporting, though it is nearly impossible to confirm. I used several publicly available databases, one estimate from *VICE News* of about how many children are enrolled in a given year in wilderness programs, and a rough estimate based on the interviews with the educational consultants, in which each consultant was asked approximately how many children they referred to such treatment programs each year.

The Growth Book given to me at Adirondack Leadership Expeditions (ALE) was supplemented by two more copies of the book, which were updated versions of my own and were given to me by Hazel and another former client. The wilderness experience described uses the interviews conducted with Hazel and are supplemented by stories gathered from further interviews with other ALE clients and the journals I kept from my time in wilderness (volumes 2,

3, 4, and 5). The story of the Oneida people is also derived from those books and outside sources. "Hurt people hurt people" was a common therapeutic refrain at the time and one I heard repeated constantly. It is the epigraph to my very first journal from that time.

reported revenues of $28 million: Jackson, Ted. "In Another Mega Deal, CRC Acquires Aspen Education." *Treatment Magazine,* October 2006. webcache.googleusercontent.com/search?q=cache%3AoDIU NNjjTAsJ%3Awww.treatmentmagazine.com%2Ffeature%2F133-in-another-mega-deal-crc-acquires-aspen-education.html%2B&cd =1&hl=en&ct=clnk&gl=us.

(estimated at 10 to 20 percent of its revenue): Story, Louise. "A Business Built on the Troubles of Teenagers." *New York Times,* August 17, 2005, Business. https://www.nytimes.com/2005/08/17/business/a-business-built-on-the-troubles-of-teenagers.html.

died from heatstroke after hiking for several hours: For the story of Matthew Meyer, see Gina Kaysen Fernandes, "Killer Camps: Another Troubled Teen Dies," HEAL, September 25, 2009. http://www.heal-online.org/killer092509.pdf.

"Residential Treatment Programs: Concerns Regarding Abuse and Death in Certain Programs for Troubled Youth," testimony before the Committee on Education and Labor, House of Representatives (statement of Gregory D. Kutz, Managing Director, Forensic Audits and Special Investigations, and Andy O'Connell, Assistant Director, Forensic Audits and Special Investigations), US Government Accountability Office (GAO), October 10, 2007: This investigation led to no known reforms among programs or had any impact on the oversight or regulation by federal or state authorities. From a sidebar provided within the testimony report (emphasis my own):

Residential treatment programs provide a range of services, including drug and alcohol treatment, confidence building, military-style discipline, and psychological counseling for troubled boys and girls with a variety of addiction, behavioral, and emotional problems. This testimony concerns programs across the country referring to themselves as wilderness therapy programs, boot camps, and academies, among other names. Many cite positive outcomes associated with specific types of residential treatment. There are also allegations regarding the abuse and death of youth enrolled in residential treatment programs. Given concerns about these allegations, particularly in reference to private programs, the Committee asked GAO to *(1) verify whether allegations of abuse and death at residential treatment programs are widespread* and (2) examine the facts and circumstances surrounding selected closed cases where a teenager died while enrolled in a private program. To achieve these objectives, GAO conducted numerous interviews and examined documents from closed cases dating as far back as 1990, including police reports, autopsy reports, and state agency oversight reviews and investigations. *GAO did not attempt to evaluate the benefits of residential treatment programs or verify the facts regarding the thousands of allegations it reviewed.* In response to questions about their efforts to define and report psychological abuse, a spokesperson wrote in an email: "The data we report on psychological or emotional maltreatment is from NCANDS. Here is a link to the NCANDS (the National Child Abuse and Neglect Data System, which is voluntary-based) database website: https://www.acf.hhs.gov/cb/research-data-technology/reporting-systems/ncands."

eighty-six since 2000: Anderson, Sulome. "When Wilderness Boot Camps Take Tough Love Too Far." *Atlantic*, August 12, 2014. https://www. theatlantic.com/health/archive/2014/08/when-wilderness-boot-camps-take-tough-love-too-far/375582/. The statistics quoted in this article come from wiki.fornits.com/, a database of behavior modification programs that has spent more than a decade chronicling the industry as a vox populi of sorts, similar to HEAL but with a more direct goal of covering the "troubled teen" industry. Forums on Reddit laud this site for its comprehensive data sets; however, the website often goes dark (it was again unavailable in December 2019), and it isn't always clear where much of the information comes from. While I was reporting for this story, a colleague at the *New York Times*, Michael Wilson, published an article titled "A Troubled School's Alarming Death Rate," on September 2, 2018, which found that students were dying at alarming rates after graduating from a residential treatment facility in Binghamton, New York, called the Family Foundation School.

Cases against Hazel's father: 9000****, 9100****, and 8800****; each case was adjudicated in New Jersey Superior Court.

Rensin, Emmett. "I Went into the Woods a Teenage Drug Addict and Came Out Sober. Was It Worth It?" First Person, *Vox*, July 7, 2016. https://www.vox.com/2016/7/7/12081150/wilderness-therapy.

Hyde, Jesse. "Life and Death in a Troubled Teen Boot Camp." *Rolling Stone*, November 12, 2015. https://www.rollingstone. com/culture/culture-news/life-and-death-in-a-troubled-teen-boot-camp-31639/.

Janofsky, Michael. "States Pressed as 3 Boys Die at Boot Camps." *New York Times*, July 15, 2001. This article contains a gem of a quote:

"'You have to provide more documents to get a fishing license than to run a camp for young boys,' said Chris Cummiskey, a Democratic state senator. 'We require nothing to demonstrate you have the qualifications to engage in this type of activity.'" Less than three months later, the *New York Times* published a special report titled "Desperate Measures: Embattled Parents Seek Help, at Any Cost," which seems to crib from Maia Szalavitz's book. That subsequent article quoted the headmaster of Swift River as saying, "I refer to some of these kids as emotional terrorists: no matter how you look at it, the home is a war zone." At the time, the programs seemed both beloved and hated, necessary but evil. Many years later, I called James Roche, the educational consultant who first suggested to my parents that I be sent away. I identified myself only as a reporter. He said he kept track of his clients. I asked him if he remembered me. He did not. I asked whether he ever referred his clients to Swift River. He remembered one, but it wasn't me. After revealing that he had prompted my parents to send me there after ALE, I asked Roche whether he felt that the conditions at Swift River during his exploratory visits made him worry for the clients, with a tuition of more than $50,000 a year. "I can only say that I didn't feel confident enough to send my clients there," he said. "I'm surprised it stayed open that long."

Solomon, Serena. "The Legal Industry for Kidnapping Teens." *Vice*, November 30, 2016. https://www.vice.com/en_us/article/jm5ng4/the-legal-industry-for-kidnapping-teens.

Krakauer, Jon. "Loving Them to Death: The Story of One Teenager's 'Wilderness Experience.'" *Outside*, October 1995.

While researching both wilderness and residential programs, I began with programs that were listed in the National Association of Therapeutic Schools and Programs (NATSAP) directory (dated 2017–18). The most common accreditation organizations were AdvancED, the Student and Exchange Visitor Information System (SEVIS), the Joint Commission (formerly JCAHO), and the Commission on Accreditation of Rehabilitation Facilities (CARF). Utah was the most common state for programs, as well as the most common licensure provider, at forty-six mentions. What else was written on accreditation was listed on the provider's web page. In seeking to determine the efficacy of such programs, journal articles included, but were not limited to: Joanna E. Bettmann, Anita R. Tucker, Julie Tracy, and Kimber J. Parry, "An Exploration of Gender, Client History, and Functioning in Wilderness Therapy Participants," *Residential Treatment for Children & Youth* 31, no. 3 (August 2014): 155–70; Kirsten L. Bolt, "Descending from the Summit: Aftercare Planning for Adolescents in Wilderness Therapy," *Contemporary Family Therapy* 38 (February 2016): 62–74; Matthew J. Hoag, Katie E. Massey, Sean D. Roberts, and Patrick Logan, "Efficacy of Wilderness Therapy for Young Adults: A First Look," *Residential Treatment for Children & Youth* 30, no. 4 (November 2013): 294–305; Keith Russell, "An Assessment of Outcomes in Outdoor Behavioral Healthcare Treatment," *Child and Youth Care Forum* 32 (December 2003): 355–81; Keith C. Russell, John C. Hendee, and Dianne Phillips-Miller, "How Wilderness Therapy Works: An Examination of the Wilderness Therapy Process to Treat Adolescents with Behavioral Problems and Addictions," in *Wilderness Science in a Time of Change Conference—Volume 3*, ed. McCool et al., Proceedings RMRS-P-15-VOL-3 (Ogden, UT: USDA, 2000), 207–17; Ebony A. Rutko and Judy Gillespie, "Where's the Wilderness in Wilderness Therapy?" *Journal of Experimental Education*, August 27, 2013, https://doi.org/10.1177/1053825913489107.

Michael A. Gass was interviewed by phone on February 14, 2018. He provided an unpublished comparison study, later published in

Children and Youth Services Review. The study "examined the longitudinal impact of Outdoor Behavioral healthcare on youth participants as reported by their parents" and found that "youth who remained in their communities were still at acute levels of psychological dysfunction," when compared to those who were admitted to outdoor treatment programs. My critique of this study is its failure to acknowledge that outdoor treatment is but one stop in a line of progressive treatments prescribed by the industry, which includes the educational consultants and residential centers. I interviewed one of his former clients, who was then a wilderness instructor at Second Nature in Utah, and also a former "troubled teen" and client of the industry.

Harakeh, Zeena, and Wilma A. M. Vollebergh. "The Impact of Active and Passive Peer Influence on Young Adult Smoking: An Experimental Study." *Drug and Alcohol Dependence*, September 26, 2011. https://www.sciencedirect.com/science/article/pii/S037687 1611003863.

Hill, Richard. "Prefrontal Cortex." *Science of Psychotherapy.* January 4, 2017. https://www.thescienceofpsychotherapy.com/prefrontal-cortex/.

National Institute on Drug Abuse (NIDA). "Brain in Progress: Why Teens Can't Always Resist Temptation." NIDA, January 27, 2015. https://www.drugabuse.gov/about-nida/noras-blog/2015/01/brain-in-progress-why-teens-cant-always-resist-temptation.

Book II: Residential

The letter excerpts that lead each chapter of this section were provided by Avery and are included in the "Averydump.pdf" collation. These letters are reprinted here, without edits, with the permission of Avery. Interviews with Avery were conducted in person in November 2017 and on November 14, 15, and 16, 2018. These interviews were supplemented by Signal phone calls and chats and Facebook Messenger exchanges over three years. The "Averydump. pdf" file provided by Avery includes letters sent and received by Avery while away at her respective programs.

college preparatory school surrounded by: My father provided me with much emailed correspondence and the Swift River program guide, which contained this description and the details on the three agreements. Further documentation, from both Avery and Hazel, came in the form of disciplinary forms, self-study evaluations, psychological evaluations, and their own correspondence between themselves and home. Photos were provided to me by a student who had graduated around the time of Avery's attendance at Swift River. Many of the students in the photos I've received, taken on disposable cameras, are now dead. The tuition amount and the comparison to Harvard is based on 2010 tuition and boarding fees and was confirmed by my father's receipts and through HEAL. Videos of graduation ceremonies, including one on August 23, 2007, were obtained by request from Berkshire Hills Productions. (Quotes from Frank are direct from the video; elsewhere, quotes from Frank and Tanya are from memory or as recalled in interviews with former clients.) Interviews with Greg were conducted by phone (unrecorded) and Facebook Messenger throughout December 2018.

of which cognitive behavioral therapy (CBT) was a part (the *Diagnostic and Statistical Manual of Mental Disorders*, 4th ed., was the most current manual during these children's stay): Hofmann, Stefan G. "Toward a Cognitive-Behavioral Classification System for Mental Disorders." *Behavior Therapy*. US National Library of Medicine, July 2014. https://www.ncbi.nlm.nih.gov/pmc/articles/PMC4234113/.

Field, T. A., E. T. Beeson, and L. K. Jones. "The New ABCs: A Practitioner's Guide to Neuroscience-Informed Cognitive-Behavior Therapy." *Journal of Mental Health Counseling* 37, no. 3 (2015): 206–20. Archived from the original (PDF) August 15, 2016; retrieved July 7, 2016. https//doi.org/10.17744/1040-2861-37.3.206.

Kiebert, Lyndsie. "Northwest Academy Closing after 24 Years." *Sandpoint Reader*, August 30, 2018. http://sandpointreader.com/northwest-academy-closing-after-24-years/.

The Synanon history section comprises research from the following sources: "Attack Therapy," Theravive, https://www.theravive.com/therapedia/attack-therapy; Aron Hillel, "The Story of This Drug Rehab–Turned–Violent Cult Is *Wild, Wild Country*–Caliber Bizarre," *Los Angeles Magazine*, April 24, 2018, https://www.lamag.com/citythinkblog/synanon-cult/; Institute of Medicine, Committee on Treatment of Alcohol Problems, *Broadening the Base of Treatment for Alcohol Problems* (Washington, DC: National Academies Press, 1990), https://doi.org/10.17226/1341; Paul Morantz, "The History of Synanon and Charles Dederich," PaulMorantz.com, 2009, http://www.paulmorantz.com/cult/the-history-of-synanon-and-charles-dederich/; Matt Novak, "Synanon's Sober Utopia: How a Drug Rehab Program Became a Violent Cult," Paleofuture, April 15, 2014, https://paleofuture.gizmodo.com/synanons-sober-utopia-how-a-drug-rehab-program-became-1562665776; Moriah Ponder, "Synanon: The Game," *Synanon Beliefs*, April 15, 2016, http://synanonbeliefs.blogspot.com/2016/04/synanonthe-game.html; Maia Szalavitz, "The Cult That Spawned the Tough-Love Teen Industry," *Mother Jones*, September/October 2007, https://www.motherjones.com/politics/2007/08/cult-spawned-tough-love-teen-industry/; Lawrence Van Gelder, "Charles Dederich, 83,

Synanon Founder, Dies," *New York Times*, March 4, 1997, https://www.nytimes.com/1997/03/04/us/charles-dederich-83-synanon-founder-dies.html.

The details about CEDU and the programs that followed are, in part, from the following sources: "Adolescent Treatment Resurgent," Special Reports, *Treatment Magazine*, April 2006, http://www.treatmentmagazine.com/special-reports/66-special-report-adolescent-addiction-treatment.html; Sarah Carr, Francesca Berardi, Zoë Kirsch, and Stephen Smiley, "These For-Profit Schools Are 'Like a Prison,'" ProPublica, March 8, 2017, https://www.propublica.org/article/these-for-profit-schools-are-like-a-prison; David A. Fox and Molly Cate, "Psychiatric Solutions and the Brown Schools Announce $63 Million Cash Deal," *Nashville Post*, February 13, 2003, https://www.nashvillepost.com/home/article/20447919/psychiatric-solutions-and-the-brown-schools-announce-63-million-cash-deal; "From CEDU to Brown Schools to Camelot Schools, Inc.," Schools Matter, May 19, 2009, http://www.schoolsmatter.info/2009/05/from-cedu-to-brown-schools-to-camelot.html; Hoda Kotb, "A Father's Quest," *NBC News*, August 1, 2005, http://www.nbcnews.com/id/8729932/ns/dateline_nbc/t/fathers-quest/#.XH-foFNKjOQ; Kathy Nussberger, "Bigger Than Life: A Personal Journey into the History of CEDU," StrugglingTeens.com, June 24, 2005, http://www.strugglingteens.com/artman/publish/article_5144.shtml; Karen J. Schwartz, "Brown Schools Reborn with $31M Shot," *Austin Business Journal*, November 9, 1997, https://www.bizjournals.com/austin/stories/1997/11/10/story1.html; Universal Health Services, Inc., *2011 Annual Report*, https://ir.uhsinc.com/static-files/5dc7e2c8-9063-4fb2-9ab3-0d961b839b15.

Pagnozzi, Amy. "About Those Tales of Elan School." *Hartford Courant*, September 25, 2018. https://www.courant.com/news/connecticut/hc-xpm-2000-07-07-0007070275-story.html.

Lifton, Robert Jay. *Thought Reform and the Psychology of Totalism*. New York: Norton, 1969.

Oyefeso, A., H. Ghodse, C. Clancy, J. Corkery, and R. Goldfinch. "Drug Abuse–Related Mortality: A Study of Teenage Addicts over a 20-Year Period." *Social Psychiatry and Psychiatric Epidemiology*. US National Library of Medicine, August 1999. https://www.ncbi.nlm.nih.gov/pubmed/10501714.

Book III: Lockdown

Excerpts from an interview with Steve in November 2017 are included as chapter introductions. In-person interviews were conducted with Mike on June 6 and December 28, 2018, and with Mark in November 2017 and on December 6, 8, and 9, 2018. Our exchanges were often cordial and heartwarming insofar as they were willing to participate in the preceding magazine and newspaper articles and the resulting book project. We chatted for hours via Signal text messages, emails, and Facebook Messenger. Mark provided his most recent arrest records and the subsequent police reports. Mike supplied testimonies from character witnesses. Their father and mother remained supportive of the reporting process until the book went to legal review and fact-checking, a response to their son's relapse. At that time, Steve requested that he not be included in the manuscript; however, his story seemed irreplaceably relevant to that of his sons' journeys, and with publicly available documents from the Federal Bureau of Investigation and the office of the US Attorney, District of New Jersey, I was able to patch holes in the boys' treatment timeline. Much of what Mike said was not easily verifiable. I reached out to Jason Finlinson for comment and never heard back. I was able to find the obituary for Joseph Dempsey II (published in the Trenton *Times* on April 30, 2015). It was nearly impossible to find conviction records for Mike, though I was able to find evidence of several arrests. When asked about the teardrops that Mike had tattooed under his eyes, normally a tattoo used to signify that someone had murdered another individual, he responded, "I lived a very authentic life."

Testing packets were from my own testing while at several of these programs.

"15 Years Later, Boy Who Vanished from Running Springs School Still Missing." *San Bernardino Sun*, June 25, 2009. http://www.sbsun.com/general-news/20090625/15-years-later-boy-who-vanished-from-running-springs-school-still-missing.

National Institute on Drug Abuse. *Principles of Adolescent Substance Use Disorder Treatment: A Research-Based Guide* (Bethesda, MD: NIDA, 2014). https://www.drugabuse.gov/publications/principles-adolescent-substance-use-disorder-treatment-research-based-guide/introduction.

———. "Is Marijuana a Gateway Drug?" (Bethesda, MD: NIDA, 2019). https://www.drugabuse.gov/publications/research-reports/marijuana/marijuana-gateway-drug.

"Academy at Ivy Ridge, New York." Help Save Troubled Teens: Teens in America are still being abused and denied constitutional rights every day at "behavior modification" programs. Accessed February

2, 2020. http://www.helpsavetroubledteens.com/academy-at-ivy-ridge-new-york.html.

Borja, Rhea R. "Brown Schools Inc. Shuts Its Doors." *Education Week*, April 13, 2005. https://www.edweek.org/ew/articles/2005/04/13/31biz.h24.html.

"Chapter 7—Bankruptcy Basics." United States Courts. Accessed February 2, 2020. https://www.uscourts.gov/services-forms/bankruptcy/bankruptcy-basics/chapter-7-bankruptcy-basics.

Bracho-Sanchez, Edith. "Nearly 1 in 7 US Kids and Teens Has a Mental Health Condition, and Half Go Untreated, Study Says." *CNN*, February 11, 2019. https://www.cnn.com/2019/02/11/health/children-teens-mental-health-untreated-study/index.html.

"Depression May Start Much Earlier than Previously Thought." *NBC News*, December 10, 2017. Video. https://www.nbcnews.com/nightly-news/video/depression-may-start-much-earlier-than-previously-thought-1113547331526.

"Preventing Suicide: Facts about Suicide." The Trevor Project. Accessed February 2, 2020. https://www.thetrevorproject.org/resources/preventing-suicide/facts-about-suicide/.

University of Utah. "Genes and Addiction." Learn. Genetics. Accessed February 2, 2020. https://learn.genetics.utah.edu/content/addiction/genes/.

Goffman, Erving. "Characteristics of Total Institutions." Accessed February 2, 2020. http://www.markfoster.net/neurelitism/totalinstitutions.pdf.

"Jean-Jacques Rousseau—The Social Contract." British Library. Accessed February 2, 2020. http://www.bl.uk/learning/histcitizen/21cc/utopia/revolution1/rousseau1/rousseau.html.

Lahey, Jessica. "The Steep Costs of Keeping Juveniles in Adult Prisons." *Atlantic*, January 8, 2016. https://www.theatlantic.com/education/archive/2016/01/the-cost-of-keeping-juveniles-in-adult-prisons/423201/.

Lohoff, Falk W. "Overview of the Genetics of Major Depressive Disorder." *Current Psychiatry Reports* 12, no. 6 (December 2010): 539–46. https://doi.org/10.1007/s11920-010-0150-6.

Melling, Joseph, Richard Adair, and Bill Forsythe. "'A Proper Lunatic for Two Years': Pauper Lunatic Children in Victorian and Edwardian England. Child Admissions to the Devon County Asylum, 1845–1914." *Journal of Social History* 31, no. 2 (1997): 371–405.

"Most Teen Psychiatric Disorders Go Untreated." *Duke Today*, November 18, 2013. https://today.duke.edu/2013/11/costello.

Shapiro, Emily. "New Clues Emerge 15 Years after Teen's Disappearance: 'We Just Want to Know He's Safe,' Family Says." *ABC News*, January 19, 2019. https://abcnews.go.com/US/clues-emerge-15-years-teens-disappearance-safe-family/story?id=60443656.

Warburton, Nicole. "Boarding School Ordered to Refund Tuition." *Deseret News*, August 19, 2005. https://www.deseret.com/2005/8/19/19907842/boarding-school-ordered-to-refund-tuition.

Nicholls, John. "Perspective: 6 Reasons Your Teen's Life Is More Stressful Than Your Own." *Washington Post*, May 15, 2017. https://www.washingtonpost.com/news/parenting/wp/2017/05/15/6-reasons-your-teens-life-is-more-stressful-than-your-own/.

O'Connor v. Donaldson, 422 U.S. 563 (1975), https://www.oyez.org/cases/1974/74-8.

Keating, Kevin. "Parents, Authorities Trying to Get to Bottom of Riot No Charges Filed after Violent Outbreak at Academy for Troubled Teens." *Spokesman-Review*, January 11, 1997. https://www.spokesman.com/stories/1997/jan/11/parents-authorities-trying-to-get-to-bottom-of/.

Drumheller, Susan. "Rocky Mountain Academy to Close." *Spokesman-Review*, February 12, 2005. https://www.spokesman.com/stories/2005/feb/12/rocky-mountain-academy-to-close/.

Semple, Kirk. "Melee Keeps Spotlight on Hard Life at Academy." *New York Times*, June 8, 2005, New York. https://www.nytimes.com/2005/06/08/nyregion/melee-keeps-spotlight-on-hard-life-at-academy.html.

Hayes, Bonnie, and Hope Hamashige. "Son Evicts Father for Living with Sex Offenders." *Los Angeles Times*, May 30, 1997. https://www.latimes.com/archives/la-xpm-1997-05-30-me-63797-story.html.

Heshmat, Shahram. "Stress and Addiction." *Psychology Today*, May 10, 2017. https://www.psychologytoday.com/blog/science-choice/201705/stress-and-addiction.

"Suicide Statistics," American Foundation for Suicide Prevention. Accessed February 16, 2016. https://afsp.org/about-suicide/suicide-statistics/.

Charles, Shamard. "Social Media Linked to Rise in Mental Health Disorders in Teens, Survey Finds." *NBC News*, March 14, 2019. https://www.nbcnews.com/health/mental-health/social-media-linked-rise-mental-health-disorders-teens-survey-finds-n982526.

"Ten Leading Causes of Death and Injury." Centers for Disease Control and Prevention. Accessed April 10, 2019. https://www.cdc.gov/injury/wisqars/LeadingCauses.html.

Dreher, Diane. "The Alarming Rise in Teen Mental Illness." *Psychology Today*, January 24, 2018. https://www.psychologytoday.com/blog/your-personal-renaissance/201801/the-alarming-rise-in-teen-mental-illness.

Tuckman, Bruce W. "Developmental Sequence in Small Groups." *Psychological Bulletin* 63, no. 6 (1965): 384–99.

Weiner, Tim. "Costa Rica Intervenes at Troubled U.S.-Owned Academy." *New York Times*, May 23, 2003, World. https://www.nytimes.com/2003/05/23/world/costa-rica-intervenes-at-troubled-us-owned-academy.html.

———. "Parents, Shopping for Discipline, Turn to Harsh Programs Abroad." *New York Times*, May 9, 2003, World. https://www.nytimes.com/2003/05/09/world/parents-shopping-for-discipline-turn-to-harsh-programs-abroad.html.

Book IV: Afterlife; or, For Forever

List of those who have died: Autopsy reports and death certificates obtained through public information requests and compiled into "death list" in research folder; all were not included in this book. Those that are included had two sources of verification: an obituary and an available death certificate.

Eisen, Lauren-Brooke. *Inside Private Prisons: An American Dilemma in the Age of Mass Incarceration.* New York: Columbia University Press, 2017.

Dr. Kristin Holland was interviewed via phone, January 12, 2018, and Lauren-Brooke Eisen was interviewed via phone, January 16, 2018. In-person interviews with several former clients across the country took place between September 2017 and November 2018. Many conversations continued through secure text messaging apps and Facebook Messenger in the years following. All, with few exceptions, were recorded.

"Troubled Kids, Troubled System." *Missoulian.* Accessed December 25, 2019. https://missoulian.com/troubled-kids-troubled-system/collection_d59fcf11-f157-5dd1-8622-0e92810e4ee7.html.

The Massachusetts state police were investigating Swift River for possible crimes of abuse: After a Freedom of Information Act request, I was able to identify the two complainants and learned what the investigators had asked the students about their time at Swift River. No further complaints were filed, and the inquiry, an ongoing investigation, seemed to dissipate. Utah DHS emails were obtained from the former student at Discovery Ranch, who emailed me over several years with her complaints and queries to the school. When I tried to confirm the inquiries with NATSAP, the accrediting board, they declined to comment. The quote from a Facebook page is of a former student who spent six weeks at a WWASPS program and who later became verbally hostile during the interview process.

Stop Child Abuse in Residential Programs for Teens Act of 2017, H.R. 3024, 115th Cong. (2017–18), congress.gov, https://www.congress. gov/bill/115thcongress/house-bill/3024/actions. This bill, which "directs the Department of Health and Human Services (HHS) to require programs designed to modify behaviors of children in a residential environment (covered programs) to prohibit child abuse and neglect and meet other specified minimum standards," was introduced but never passed.

Epilogue

Survivor Facebook group ASR Connection: This is one of the many groups in which former clients from these programs meet to discuss their time away and their respective programs and to share news updates about friends they had at the programs and have since lost. ASR Connection is home base specifically for those who attended the Academy at Swift River. It is where I began noticing that many of the boys and girls with whom I had attended these programs were dying, as people posted their obituaries or links to Facebook pages marked "remembering."

a white brick building advertised on commuter rails and billboards: The description of Carrier Clinic comes from my five days there before my family's insurance coverage ran out.

It is a police code: 601 doesn't seem to be a universal police radio code referring to juvenile offenses/offenders, but it is in certain areas, such as the state of California and the city of Tempe, Arizona (http://s3.amazonaws.com/zanran_storage/forums.radioreference. com/ContentPages/2546713456.pdf).

ACKNOWLEDGMENTS

My sincerest gratitude to MacDowell, the Banff Centre for Arts and Creativity, and the Logan Nonfiction Fellowship program at the Carey Institute for Global Good, for their gifts of time, fellowship, and nature; to the Fund for American Studies in Washington, DC, for its much-needed financial support; to the Harry Frank Guggenheim Foundation with John Jay's Center on Media, Crime and Justice; and the former Schuster Institute for Investigative Journalism at Brandeis University, for their research assistance and support.

My greatest appreciation to John Stauffer, who inspired and elevated my prose by providing a list of provoking and moving books and who sat with me in Cambridge, Massachusetts, and on distant phone calls for hours spent discussing the finer points of narrative writing, talks that rank highest among my life's treasures.

For their guidance, editing, fact-checking, legal review, support, representation, encouragement, advisement, and friendship, I offer ardent thanks to everyone at Little A, Joshuah Bearman, Jared Bland, Lisa Button, Dan Crissman, Kathy Daneman, Sarah Fallon, Marc Feldman, Christy Fletcher, Josh Friedman, Sarah Fuentes, Florence Graves, Gregory Giuliana, Michael Harris, Frank Huyler, Tom Jennings, Brett Kaplan, Steve Kenny, Jason Kwan, my colleagues at the *New York Times*, Katherine Reynolds Lewis, Steve McElroy, Kimberly Meyer, Erin Calligan Mooney, Heather Mooney, Sabrina Negrón, Susan Orlean,

Sharad Raghu, Noah Rosenberg, Carol Shaben, Michael Shapiro, Sonja Sharp, Brendan Spiegel, Kara Stanley, Farah Stockman, Remy Tumin, Nick Quinn, and Jamie Wolf.

I am indebted to my father; my mother; my (little) twin sister; ed Elettra: *con te trovo bellezza duratura ovunque, un mondo perfetto che abbiamo creato insieme.*

For their help and patience while unburdening me of my ignorance and partial recollections, I am grateful for Hazel, Avery, Mark, Mike, and their families, for the commitment of their time and generosity as I unearthed portions of their lives that had long been left dormant and unsettled.

And, not least of all, to those whose lives inspired this book, those who I roomed with and met over days and weeks and months of tired anguish, those who did not live to see its publication.

ABOUT THE AUTHOR

Photo © 2018 Sharona Jacobs

Kenneth R. Rosen has written for the *New Yorker*, the *New York Times Magazine*, *VQR*, and the *Atlantic*. He is a contributing writer at *WIRED* and the author of *Bulletproof Vest*. He spent six years at the *New York Times*, his hometown newspaper, and now divides his time between northern Italy and Massachusetts. For more information, visit www.kennethrrosen.com.